# AN AUTHENTICATED HISTORY OF THE FAMOUS BELL WITCH

# AN AUTHENTICATED HISTORY OF THE FAMOUS BELL WITCH

MARTIN VAN BUREN INGRAM

**WILDSIDE PRESS**

An Authenticated History of the Famous Bell Witch

Published in 2009 by Wildside Press.
www.wildsidepress.com

# Preface

It is not the purpose of the writer to present a romance for the entertainment of lovers of fiction, nor to establish a theory to please the fancy of adherents of so-called theosophy, but simply to record events of historical fact, sustained by a powerful array of incontrovertible evidence, as it comes to hand, testifying to the most wonderful phenomenon the world has any account of a visitation known as the "Bell Witch," believed at the time by many to have been of supernatural origin; which appeared in Robertson County, Tennessee, some seventy-five years ago, inflicting unendurable suffering on John Bell, the head of the family, and was said to have ended his life and which also awakened a sensation that has lived through a generation. The writer is aware of the fact that the average person of today eschews the belief in the existence of witches, ghosts, and apparitions, as a relic of past superstition, and as a subject for ridicule; nevertheless, spectres stalk the earth today just as they did hundreds of years ago, the only difference being that we now place a different interpretation upon them, calling them spirits, fantasies, psychic manifestations, etc., instead of ghosts and witches, and people who laugh at the superstition of our fathers only need be put to the test to prove this fact. However, this is not the place for moralizing, nor will the writer find any occasion for drawing on his imagination for a vivid description of goblins and devils incarnate, or for painting the revelry of unknown demons on a mission of torment, to, make the hair Stand on one's head, or cause the unregenerated to shun neglected grave yards. This part of the story is told by others who mingled with the familiar spirits, held conversation with the invisible, took part in their worship, participated in the ghost dances and midnight revelries, held councils with the spooks, witnessed the jack-a-lantern performances, saw unshapely sights and horrifying transformations, and felt the warm blood curdle in their veins.

The author only assumes to compile the data, formally presenting the history of this greatest of all mysteries, just as the matter is furnished to hand, written by Williams Bell, a member of the family, some fifty-six years ago, together with other corroborative testimony by men and women of irreproachable character and unquestionable veracity.

It may be a strange story, never theirs it is authentic, not only as recorded by Williams Bell, but transmitted to the present generation of the surrounding country through family reminiscences of that most eventful and exciting period of the century which set hundreds of people to investigating, including Gen. Andrew Jackson, and is recognized in every household as a historical truth.

No one denies or doubts the existence of witchcraft, etc., during the dark ages, and it may be accepted as equally true, that just as enlightened Christianity has progressed, the deviltry of the past decades has kept pace with the advancement, in transformations, assuming other forms and new channels for mystifying people; such as spiritual séances, mind reading, hypochondria, hypnotism, electrical phenomena, etc.; to satisfy that innate theosophy of the human family, or idle desire to comprehend unrevealed mysteries of God and nature. However this may be, there is not one person in a thousand who does not hold to some kind of superstition, and those most given to ridiculing the belief in witchcraft of past ages, believe in omens, prognostics, dreams and revelations. They carry a rabbit's foot or buckeye, keep a horse shoe over or under the door, see spectres stalking around a table of thirteen, or could not be induced to start a journey or begin any work on Friday, and since people of the present day cannot explain the phenomena in spiritual manifestations, mind reading, electric wonders, etc., their ancestors may be excused for believing in witchcraft, inasmuch as they accepted the. Bible for the guidance of their faith and believed all it says on this subject, as they did that pertaining to the soul's salvation, and sought to put away witchcraft, that Christianity might prevail.

—M. V. INGRAM

# Chapter 1

## *Introduction*

Before entering upon an investigation or going into details of the acts and demonstrations of the Bell Witch, it is proper that the reader should know something of the Bell family and citizens of the community who witnessed the manifestations, expended their energies in trying to discover the origin and force of the phenomena, and who in connection with the Bell family, give credence to the truth of these statements. The story will not be altogether new to thousands who have heard graphic accounts from the lips of the old people who witnessed the excitement and have, perhaps, also read short newspaper sketches. No full or authentic account, however, has ever been published. Newspapers were few and far between at the time these events transpired, and there were no enterprising reporters or novelists abroad in the land. Several writers in later years undertook to compile the story, but could not obtain the authentic details. Williams Bell, it seems, was the only one who kept a diary of what transpired, which he put in shape in 1846, twenty-six years after the culmination of the tragic events in the death of John Bell, Sr. It appears also that he was inspired to write the sketch by the intensity of the living sensation that sent a tremor through every nerve of his body, as it kept fresh in the memory of everyone, the astounding manifestations that continued to be rehearsed at every fireside and in every social gathering, taking on new phases and versions far from the truth. Some enterprising person, wise in his own conceit, undertook to solve the mystery, and failing to arrive at any satisfactory conclusion, gave currency to a suspicion that the young daughter, Betsy Bell, actuated by her brothers, John and Drewry, was the author of the demonstration, and that the purpose was to make money by the exhibitions. This version found lodgment in many minds not acquainted with the facts, and the discussion became very distasteful and irritating to the family, and Williams Bell determined to write the incidents and truth of the whole story and let the public pass upon the injustice of such a judgment. After it was written, the brothers consulted over the matter, and finally for good reasons then existing, agreed not to publish the statement during the life of any member of John Bell, Sr.'s immediate family. Williams Bell died a few years after, this, and gave the manuscript to his eldest son, James Allen Bell, who has carefully preserved it. The writer was raised within a few miles of the Bell place, and has been familiar with the witch story from his youth up, and becoming intimately acquainted with Joel and Allen Bell during his residence in Springfield, about 1867 applied to Joel Bell for the privilege of writing the history then, while himself, sister Betsy, Frank Miles, Lawson Fort, Patrick McGowen, Johnson, and others acquainted with the facts, were still living. Joel Bell assented to the proposition, but Allen Bell declined to furnish his father's manuscript, and the matter was dropped until recently. Since the death of all of the family who were victims of the frightful disturbance, Allen Bell has consented to the use of his father's statement in connection with other testimony. The further explanation of the Publication of the history of these stirring events, after the lapse of many years, will be found in the following correspondence:

ADAIRVILLE, KY.
July 1st, 1891

M. V. Ingram, Esq.,
Clarksville, Tenn.:

DEAR SIR — Some years ago, while you were engaged in publishing a newspaper at Springfield, Tenn., Uncle Joel Bell applied to me for the manuscript of my father, Williams Bell, stating that the application was made at your request for the purpose of incorporating the same in a full and complete history of the so-called Bell Witch, which proposition I declined to accede to at that time, for several reasons that need not now be mentioned. However, one objection was, that after writing his own memories, and the recollections of other members of the family, father consulted with Uncle John Bell in regard to the matter, and they determined that in view of all the surrounding circumstances, it was best that it should not be published during the life of any of Grandfather John Bell's immediate family, and he gave me all of his notes just before his death with this injunction. So many painfully abhorrent misrepresentations had gone out concerning the mystery that he desired the writing should be preserved, that the truth might be known in after years, should the erroneous views which had found lodgment concerning the origin of the distress continue to live through tradition handed down to an enlightened generation under a version so disparaging. This history was written by father during the Fall and Winter of 1846, and is the only sketch ever written in detail by any one cognizant of the facts and demonstrations. Now, nearly seventy-five years having elapsed, the old members of the family who suffered the torments having all passed away, and the witch story still continues to be discussed as widely as the family name is known, under misconception of the facts, I have concluded that in justice to the memory of an honored ancestry, and to the public also whose minds have been abused in regard to the matter, it would be well to give the whole story to the World. You having made the application years ago, and believing you are capable, and will if you undertake it, being already acquainted with many of the circumstances, compile a faithful history of the events, I am willing to let you have this manuscript and notes, on the condition that you will agree to include all other corroborative testimony still to be had, and write a deserved sketch of Grandfather John Bell and family, and those associated with him in any way during the period of the unexplained visitation which afflicted him and gave rise to the excitement.

Respectfully,
J.A. BELL

CLARKSVILLE, TENN.
July 5th, 1891

Hon. J. Allen Bell,
Adairville, Ky.:

DEAR SIR — In reply to your favor of the 1st inst., I remember distinctly the discussion between Mr. Joel E. Bell and myself in 1867, in regard to the publication of the history of the Bell Witch, and also his after report of the interview with you, which caused the matter to be dropped. Joel Bell was a gentleman whom I esteemed very highly for his moral worth and generous friendship. His earnestness impressed me with the views so decidedly expressed in favor of the publication then, believing the facts would correct the erroneous impressions which had been created. I will accept your proposition and undertake to compile such testimony as may still exist; as you suggest, and will endeavor to make a faithful record of the facts. I have always regarded the so-called Bell Witch as a phenomenon for which the Bell family, who suffered the infliction and misfortune, could in no wise be responsible, but were entitled to all of that sympathy so generously bestowed by the good people of that community who knew John Bell only to honor him. But in undertaking the work, it shall not be my purpose to account for the series of dramatic events that so confused and mystified people at that time, but compile the data and let readers form their own conclusion. I believe the publication will do good, not only in correcting a false impression, but will recount historical events and facts concerning the most remarkable visitations, in the early part of the present century, that ever afflicted any community, giving the present generation some idea of the grounds for the superstition that possessed the early settlers of this country.

Very truly, your friend,
M. V. INGRAM

# Chapter 2

*The Early Settlers — Society and Religion —*
*Kate the Witch — The Bell Family —*
*The School Master and Betsy's First Lover*

More than one hundred years ago, the Star of Empire took its course westward, following the footprints of the advance guard who had blazed the way with blood, driving the red man, whose savagery rendered life unsafe and civilization impossible, from this great country, then, as now, teeming with possibilities. Couriers carried back the glad tidings of peace and safety, and a glowing account of the rich lands, fine forests, great water courses — rivers, creeks, brooks, and bubbling springs. In short, the land of milk and honey had been discovered in Tennessee, then the far west, and the flow of emigration from North Carolina, Virginia, and other old States, became steady and constant, rapidly settling up the country. They were of the best blood of the land; men of brawn and brain. They came with the axe, the hoe, the plow and sickle. They brought with them their customs and notions of civilization and Christianity, having the Bible and the American Constitution for their guide. Wild speculations and schemes of laying out great, cities and building railroads, had not entered the dreams of men then. Good lands and farming was the object, and only young men of muscle, nerve, honesty of purpose, and a courageous disposition to work, possessed of self-reliance and frugal habits, were among the immigrants.

Along with this tide of immigration came John Bell and his amiable wife Lucy and family of promising children, also a number of likely Negroes, then slaves. They landed with their train of wagons and splendid teams in the west end of Robertson county, Tennessee, near where Adams Station is now located, on the Southeastern line of the Louisville & Nashville Railroad, in the year 1804, and met with a hearty reception by old friends who had preceded them. There was general rejoicing in the community over the accession to the quiet happy neighbor hood. Mr. Bell purchased a home partially improved, with good houses, barns, and a fine young orchard, surrounding himself with about one thousand acres of the best land on Red River; and settled down for life, clearing more land and opening a large and fertile farm. His commanding appearance, steadfast qualities, and force of character, at once gave him rank and influence in the community. Mrs. Lucy Bell was an exemplary mother among matrons, ruling her children with the glowing passion of a tender loving mother's heart; even the stern husband yielded to every glance of her gentle piercing eyes and loving smiles. Everybody was in love with Mrs. Bell, and wondered at the power of her influence, and the charming discipline exercised in her home. It was indeed a happy and very prosperous family, as everyone recognized.

The principal families composing this delightful neighborhood at that time were Rev. James and Rev. Thomas Gunn, the pioneers of Methodism; William Johnson and James Johnson, the founder of Johnson's Camp Ground, and his two sons, John and Calvin Johnson; John Bell, Jerry Batts, the Porters, Frederick Batts, the Long family, James Byrns, the Gardners, Bartletts and Dardens, the Gooch family, Pitman, Ruffin, Mathews, Morris, Frank Miles and brothers, "Ninety-Six" Needham, Justice and Chester; and just across Red River, between that and Elk Fork Creek, was the large Fort settlement, the Sugg family, McGowen, Bourne, Royster, Waters, Thomas Gorham, Herring, and many other good people. Rev. Sugg Fort was a pioneer Baptist minister and a man of great influence. These people raised large families, and formed the aristocratic society of the country, and no man whose character for morality and integrity was not above reproach was admitted to the circle. The circle, however, widened, extending up and down the river, and into Kentucky, embracing a large area of territory. Open hospitality characterized the community, and neighbors assisted each other and co-operated in every good move for the advancement of education and Christianity. They established schools, built churches and worshipped together. Churches took the name of the river, creek or spring of the location, and it was nothing uncommon for people to go ten or fifteen miles to church and visiting. The Baptist took the lead in building houses of worship, Red River Church being the first established in that community, which was in 1791. It still maintains the name and organization under the control of a new generation, but has changed the location, moving a short distance to Adams Station, building a new and more commodious house. Drake's Pond Church on the State line, one mile east of Guthrie, Ky., was the next congregation of worshippers organized. This church was held by the Predestinarian Baptist when the split took place in the denomination later. Rev. Sugg Fort was pastor of both churches, and the two congregations visited and worshipped with each other a great deal, the churches being only seven miles apart. The Methodists, in the meanwhile, established several churches in the circle, presided over by Rev. James and Rev. Thomas Gunn, who itinerated a wide scope of country, evangelizing with great success, and it was not uncommon for them to travel fifty miles to marry a couple or preach a funeral. The people of the Bell neighborhood were about equally divided in their church affiliations between the Baptist and Methodist, but toleration, Christian fellowship, and a spirit of emulation prevailed. They worshipped together, and the ties of friendship grew and strengthened; families intermarried, and these fond relations still exist in the present generation.

Like all new countries, the settlement became infested with robbers and horse thieves, and it was almost impossible for any one to keep a good horse. It seemed that the legal authorities were powerless to detect and break up the vandalism and the situation necessitated some active measures on the part of the citizens. Nicholas Darnley, who lived on the Tennessee side of Drake's Pond, several of the Forts and Gunns, taking the matter in hand, quietly organized a large vigilance committee to ferret out such crimes, and were not long in detecting the criminals. The ring leaders of the band proved to be men connected with respectable families; one lived in the bend of Red River below Port Royal, and the other a highly connected citizen of Kentucky. The regulators took the two thieves into the dense forest and swamps between Drake's Pond and Sadlersville (as now known), strung them up to limbs of trees and whipped them from head to foot with keen switches. The men were then set free, and warned that if caught again after three days they would be hung. The thieves emigrated at once, crossing the Mississippi River, and finally settled in Louisiana, reformed, leading more honorable lives, and soon became extensive cotton planters and died respected, leaving handsome fortunes. Both raised large families, ignorant of this stain, and therefore their names are prudently withheld from this sketch, but the circumstance, which was not very uncommon in olden times, illustrates the fact, that the hickory used by our fathers was more potent in correcting bad morals than the penitentiaries of today, and was not less humane. Convicts who darken the door of a modern prison, suffer the same character of punishment, laid on with greater brutality, and other cruelties, and rarely is one ever reclaimed. Whatever may be said of the barbarity of the old whipping post law, it was certain punishment for the convicted, and a greater terror to lawbreakers, than the penitentiaries of the present day, and was more effective in every way, giving bad men a chance to reform. No criminal cared to show his face in the community after going to the whipping post.. They invariably moved and led better lives.

The principal trading points for this locality at that time were Port Royal, Tenn., and Keysburg, Ky., the oldest towns in this country and just as large then as now; also Adairville, Ky., 8pringfield, Clarksville, and Nashville, Tenn. Merchants bought their goods in Philadelphia and New Orleans, hauling them out by wagons until steamboats were brought into use. People, how ever, bought but very few goods. They raised cotton and flax, sheep for wool, and made their clothing at home, using the hand gin, cards, spinning wheel, and old-fashioned loom, and had a cobbler to make up the hides, tanned in a neighboring tannery on shares, into shoes. Doctors were scarce in the country, and the few located at the trading points, did the medical practice of the entire country, riding from five to fifteen miles to see patients.

Some twelve years have passed since John Bell commenced a happy and prosperous career in his new home on the south bank of Red River in Robertson County. A very interesting family of children have grown up, and fortune has smiled on him at every turn. He has become one of the wealthiest and most influential men in the community, respected for his integrity of character, Christian devotion and generous hospitality. His house had become the home of every passing stranger, and neighbors delighted in frequent calls and visits. Many were the pleasant social gatherings at the Bell Place, in which Prof. Richard Powell, the handsome bachelor school teacher, found pleasurable mingling. He was a man of culture and force of character, distinguished in his profession, which was a high calling at that day and time. Everyone liked Dick Powell for his fine social qualities and genial manners. He kept a large school in the settlement, and was the educator of several of Mr. Bell's children, especially his young daughter Betsy, whom he gave four years of tuition, and relished every opportunity for praising her virtues to her mother, telling Mrs. Bell what a bright, sweet girl she was, and no one was disposed to controvert his judgment on this point. Betsy was now ripening into lovely girlhood, and the lads who had grown up with her under Richard Powell's tutorship, were as firmly impressed with her charms as was the teacher. However, the boys were yet a little shy of any demonstrations giving expression to their convictions, as Betsy was considered too young to receive the attention of beaux, and bashful youngsters made excuses for calling at Mr. Bell's to visit his boys. There was one very gallant youth, however, who made no effort to disguise his admiration for the blue-eyed beauty, and his attentions to Betsy were not discouraged. Joshua Gardner was a very handsome young man, graceful in appearance and cultured in manners, and very entertaining socially. He was of a good family, and had won the distinction of being the sprightliest youth in School. Everyone conceded that Josh was a fine fellow, who would make his way in the world, and his attentions to Betsy were not displeasing to the old folks nor her brothers.

About this time a mysterious visitor, claiming to hale from the old North State, put in appearance, taking up headquarters at John Bell's, and persisted, in spite of opposition, in remaining indefinitely to fulfill certain missions. This was "Kate" the witch, which the reader is doubtless growing very impatient to know something about. The first evidence of the mystery, or the appearance of things out of ordinary course of events, occurred in 1817. Mr. Bell, while walking through his corn field, was confronted by a strange animal, unlike any he had ever seen, sitting in a corn row, gazing steadfastly at him as he approached nearer. He concluded that it was probably a dog, and having his gun in hand, shot at it, when the animal ran off. Some days after, in the late afternoon, Drew Bell observed a very large fowl, which he supposed to be a wild turkey, as it perched upon the fence, and ran in the house for a gun to kill it. As he approached within shooting distance, the bird flapped its wings and sailed off, and then he was mystified in discovering that it was not a turkey, but some unknown bird of extraordinary size. Betsy walked out one evening soon after this with the children among the big forest trees near the house, and saw something which she described as a pretty little girl dressed in green, swinging to a limb of a tall oak. Then came Dean, the servant, reporting that a large black dog came in the road in front of him at a certain place, every night that he visited his wife Kate, who belonged to Alex Gunn, and trotted along before him to the cabin door and then disappeared.

These strange apparitions, however, passed for the time unnoticed, exciting no apprehensions whatever. Very soon there came a strange knocking at the door and on the walls of the house, which could not be detected. Later on the disturbance commenced within the house; first in the room occupied by the boys and appeared like rats gnawing the bed posts, then like dogs fighting, and also a noise like trace chains dragging over the floor. As soon as a candle was lighted to investigate the disturbance, the noise would cease, and screams would be heard from Betsy's room; something was after her, and the girl was frightened nearly out of her life.

Mr. Bell now felt a strange affliction coming on him, which he could not account for. It was stiffness of the tongue, which came suddenly, and for a time, when these ·spells were on, he could not eat. He described it as feeling like a small stick of wood crosswise in his mouth, pressing out both cheeks, and when he attempted to eat it would push the victuals out of his mouth.

John Bell endured such things for a long time, perhaps a year or more, hoping that the disturbance would cease, charging his family to keep the matter a profound secret and they were loyal in their obedience. As frightful as were the demonstrations, not a single neighbor or friend outside of the family had any knowledge of the facts until the affliction became insufferable when Mr. Bell, in strict confidence, laid the matter before James Johnson and wife, narrating the circumstances, insisting that they should spend a night at his house, hoping that Mr. Johnson could throw some light on the mystery. The wish was very cordially acceded to and at the hour of retirement Mr. Johnson led in family worship, as was his custom, reading a chapter, singing a hymn, and then offering prayer. He prayed very earnestly and fervently for a revelation of the cause, or that the Lord would remove the disturbance. As soon as all were in bed and the lights extinguished, the frightful racket commenced, and presently entered Mr. and Mrs. Johnson's room with increased demonstrations, stripping the cover from their bed. Mr. Johnson was astounded and sat upright in bed in wild amazement; but he was a man of strong faith and cool courage, and recovering from the confusion he collected his wits and commenced talking to the spectre, adjuring it to reveal itself and tell for what purpose it was there. The effect of the entreaty convinced Mr. Johnson that the demonstrations came from an intelligent source of some character, but beyond this he had no conception whatever. He however insisted that Mr. Bell should let the matter be known, and call in other friends to assist in the further investigation. This was agreed to, and there was no end to the number of visitors and investigations. Kate, however, developed more rapidly, and soon in answer to the many entreaties, commenced talking, and among the first vocal demonstrations, repeated Mr. Johnson's song and prayer offered on the night of his first visit, referred to, word for word, personating the old gentleman, assimilating his character so perfectly that no one could distinguish it from his voice and prayer.

Kate had now become a fixture, attaining eminence as chief among citizens, at home in the excellent family of John Bell, Sr., and distinguished as the Bell Witch. He, she, or it — whatever may have been the sex, has never been divined — made great pretentious for religion taking Mr. Johnson for a model of Christianity, calling him "Old Sugar Mouth," frequently observing "Lord Jesus, how sweet old Sugar Mouth prays; how I do love to hear him." Kate delighted in scriptural controversies, could quote any text or passage in the

Bible, and was able to maintain a discussion With the ablest theologians, excelling in fervency of prayer and devotional songs — no human Voice was sweet. Kate made frequent visits to North Carolina, John Bell's old neighborhood, never absent longer than a day or an hour, but always reporting correctly the news or events of the day in that vicinity. With all of these excellent traits of character, Kate behaved badly toward visitors and all members of the family except Mrs. Lucy Bell, to whom the witch was devoted, declaring that "Old Luce" was a good Woman, but manifesting very great aversion for "Old Jack" — John Bell, Sr. He was most detestable and loathsome in the eyes of Kate, for which no cause was ever assigned. But the witch often declared its purpose of killing him before leaving the place.

Kate was also averse to the growing attachment between Joshua Gardner and Betsy Bell, and remonstrated, punishing Betsy severely in divers ways for receiving his devoted attentions. Esther, Betsy's older and only sister, married Bennett Porter, just before the witch had fully developed, and Betsy was now the pride and pet of the household. Like all other girls, however, she made bosom companions of two of her female associates. These were Theny Thorn and Rebecca Porter. They were Betsy's seniors by one or two years, but were both vivacious, charming girls, and had many admirers. Becky Porter was a sister of Bennett Porter, and Theny Thorn was the adopted daughter of James Johnson and second wife, also a niece of Mrs. Johnson, who had no children, and they were greatly devoted to her. In fact she was petted and almost spoilt, and knew them only as father and mother. The three girls were classmates in school, close neighbors, the families all on the most intimate terms, and they grew up together like sisters, almost inseparably attached to each other, going together in society, and were the chief attraction for all the young men in the country. Especially was young James Long devoted to charming Becky Porter, and Alex Gooch felt a strong pulsation in his heart for lovely Theny Thorn.

Kate the Witch never slept, was never idle or confined to any place, but was here and there and everywhere, like the mist of night or the morning sunbeams, was everything and nothing, invisible yet present, spreading all over the neighborhood, prying into everybody's business and domestic affairs; caught on to every ludicrous thing that happened, and all of the sordid, avaricious meanness that transpired; divining the inmost secrets of the human heart, and withal, was a great blabber mouth; getting neighbors by the ears, taunting people with their sins and shortcomings, and laughing at their folly in trying to discover the identity of the mystery. Kate, however, held fast to Christianity, and was a regular fire-eating Methodist while associating with "Old Sugar Mouth" and his son, Calvin Johnson; was a regular attendant at Mr. Johnson's prayer meetings; calling the amens, thumping on the chairs, and uttering the exclamation "Lord Jesus."

People now concluded that a good spirit had been sent to the community to work wonders and prepare the good at heart for the second advent. Kate's influence was something like that exercised over a "whiskey-soaked town" by Rev. Sam Jones at the present day, only more forceful. The sensation spread hundreds of miles and people were wild with the excitement, and traveled long distances on horseback and in vehicles to witness the demonstrations, and Mr. Bell's home was continually overflowing with visitors and investigators. John Bell's hospitality, however, was equal to the great strain. He fed all visitors free of charge. Citizens of the community soon learned to respect. Kate's presence and councils, as they feared and abominated the witch's scorpion tongue. Everybody got good; the wicked left off swearing, lying and whiskey drinking, just ns people do now for Rev. Sam Jones. The avaricious were careful not to covet or lay hands on that which belonged to their neighbors, lest Kate might tell on them. No man allowed his right hand to do anything that the left might be ashamed of. No citizen thought of locking his smoke house or crib door, or of staying up through the night to guard his hen roost or watermelon patch. Negroes were too sleepy to leave their cabins after night, and white people went out only in companies after dark to attend prayer meetings. The wickedest man in the country could break new ground all day with a fiery team and kicking colts, singing psalms, and never think of cursing, though he might be laid out in a trance a dozen times by a punch from the frisky plow handles. No incident out of the regular routine of every day transactions occurred that the witch did not know all about the affair, and would tell the circumstance to someone in less than an hour.

What a great factor in politics this warlock would be at the present time? The whole country would vote Kate an honorary life membership of both houses of Congress, and the right to preside in all departments at Washington, with the privilege of compelling witnesses, books, papers, and giving reports to the newspapers. The witch might also spread out over the entire land during election times to warn the people who was fit for office. If so, only those commended by the mage would ever attain to office, for no amount of money could bribe the witch to conceal the schemes and purposes of designing men. Whatever else may be said of the Bell

Witch, Kate evinced an exalted opinion and profound respect for an honest man, and never hesitated, when occasion seemed to require, to remark the distinction of character in men, as in the case of the two brothers, John and Calvin Johnson. John was pronounced a sly trickster, frank and genial in his outward appearance and association, but secretly planning in his own mind some crafty scheme to detect the mysterious oracle. Calvin, however, was an honest man with a pure heart, free from guile, and he was permitted to feel the gentle pressure of the seer's velvety hand, which, when laid on others, produced a smarting sensation, like the chastising palm of an irate mother when laid on a disobedient boy. However, this semblance of deep piety did not hold out. It answered a good purpose in the prayer meetings, serving to promote Christian Fellowship and unify different denominations in devotional exercises, in alternate meetings at Brother Johnson's (Methodist), and Brother Bell's (Baptist) but Kate at last undertook too much for the most renowned wizard. Satan, it is said, was once a respected angel, and becoming too presumptuous, fell from his high state, and so from the same kind of rashness Kate "tumbled." This came of attending the preaching of Rev. James Gunn and Rev. Sugg Fort, thirteen miles apart; on the same day and same hour, trying to reconcile the Arminianism of the one and Calvinism of the other, mixing Methodist fire with Baptist water. This was too much even for so great an oracle as the Bell Witch. The preachers were all right, and their sermons and doctrines both got taken one at the time, and a regenerated person could, hardly miss heaven on either line, but it would perplex an angel, much less a presumptuous zealot, to run on both schedules at the same time. This is what Kate undertook to do, and succeeded to the extent of taking in both sermons; but the mixture was too strong for the Witch's faith, and the whole stock of piety was soon worked out at a discount. After this Kate backslid and fell from grace, took up with unregenerated spirits, held high carnivals at John Gardner's still house, coming in very drunk, cursing and fuming, filling the house with bad breath, spitting on the Negroes, overturning the chairs, stripping the cover from the beds, pinching and slapping the children, and teasing Betsy in every conceivable way and to such an alarming extent that her parents feared for her to remain alone in her room a single night, and when it was not convenient for Theny Thorn or Rebecca Porter, or both to stay with her, they sent her from home to spend the night. This is something of the general character of Kate, the unknown citizen, which is authentically recorded in detail by Williams Bell and others further on.

# Chapter 3

## *Biographical Sketch of the Bell Family and Reminiscences*

John Bell, Sr., was born in 1750 in Halifax County, North Carolina. He was a son of William Bell, a thrifty farmer and prominent citizen. John was given a good country, school education, and was brought up on the farm, where he acquired industrious and steady habits in youth, and grew to manhood noted for his indomitable energy and perseverance, combining all of those good qualities which fits a man for usefulness and success in life, coupled with good practical sense and a keen quick perception. In the meantime he learned the cooper's business, which was a valuable trade at that day, and with all he was a handsome, prepossessing gentlemen.

In 1782 John Bell wedded Miss Lucy Williams, daughter of John Williams of Edgecombe County, North Carolina, a man of considerable wealth and prominence in the community. Lucy was a very handsome, winsome lady, possessing those higher qualities of mind and heart and grace of manners which go to make up that lovely female character she developed all through life, as the reader has already been informed. John Williams approved the match, and gave his daughter a young Negro woman, Chloe, and her child, named Dean, and with the means John had saved up, they bought a farm in Edgecombe County, beginning a prosperous career. They both embraced the Baptist faith and became earnest Christian workers, living up to their religion through life.

Twenty-two years of prosperity having now attended the happy union, John Bell and wife found a large family growing up around them — six children had been born to them, and Chloe had eight, that had become valuable as slaves — a family of seventeen. There was absolute necessity for more elbow room; more land to give their boys a chance in life. Then it was that Mr. Bell determined to emigrate to Robertson county, Tenn., settling, as he did, on Red River, some forty miles north of Nashville, which history the reader is already familiar with.

At the time the remarkable events in this history begun, they had nine children, seven sons and two daughters: Jesse, John, Jr., Drewry, Benjamin, Esther, Zadok, Elizabeth, Richard Williams and Joel Egbert. Benjamin died young; Zadok was educated for the bar, and became a brilliant lawyer. He settled in Alabama, and died in the flush of young manhood, having a promising future before him. The other seven lived to mature age, honored and useful citizens.

John Bell made it a rule to owe no man. He paid as he went, and accumulated rapidly from his farm by economy in management. He was always forehanded, having money ahead, and was accommodating to his neighbors, who were not so fortunate. He was as firm in his convictions as he was dignified in character and generous in hospitality, consequently he was a tower of strength in the community. His sons and daughters, and the present generation of grandchildren, have been no less honored, and no family name has made a stronger impress on that county.

The first marriage in the family was that of Esther, who wedded Alex Bennett Porter, July 24th, 1817, Rev. Thomas Gunn officiating at the altar. Esther was a very prepossessing young lady, gifted with many graces and charms which made her attractive. Bennett Porter was also popular, and the wedding was quite a noted event. Jesse Bell, the eldest son, married Miss Martha Gunn, daughter of Rev. Thomas Gunn. This marriage took place several months later. Both couples settled in the neighborhood, making a fair start in life, sharing the confidence and good will of the community. A year or two after the death of John Bell, Sr., the two families emigrated to Panola County, Miss., where they settled for life and raised large and interesting families, and have many descendants there at present. John Bell, Jr., the second son, was said to be the very image of his father, and developed the old gentleman's character to a great degree, and was distinguished for his firmness and stern integrity. He was a successful, farmer and a progressive citizen, and enjoyed the fullest confidence of the community. He served as magistrate during a term of years. John Bell, Jr., married Elizabeth Gunn, daughter of Rev. Thomas Gunn, and raised an interesting family. He died in 1861. John, Jr., Drew, and Alex Gunn engaged in flat boating in 1815. They built generally two or three boats during the summer season, in Red River, at Thomas Gorham's, now known as the Sugg mill place. The boats were constructed of rough hewn and sawed timber, and were cabled to the bank, awaiting the Winter or Spring rise in the water, when they were loaded with all kinds of produce, tobacco, flour, corn, oats, bacon, whiskey, dried fruits, butter, turkeys, chickens, eggs, etc., and were cut loose on the first current of sufficient tide to float the crafts out, each boat having two men at the oars and the captain at the stern with one oar, to steer the boat in the proper current to avoid snags and breakers, as the craft drifted on with the flow to the great Father of Waters, and down to

New Orleans, the southern mart. This was the only way people had at that time for shipping their produce to market, except by wagons. It was very slow, but generally sure, and always got there with the tide that left Red River. Each one of the partners would take charge of a boat as captain or master, and first loaded, first off. After arriving at New Orleans, and selling the cargo, the boats were worthless except for fuel or second-hand lumber, and they were sold for what the timber would bring, and the boatmen made their way home as best they could, generally walking, and arriving in time to build more boats for the next season. A bill of lading for the last one of these trips, still in existence, was made out to Alex Gunn, April 1818, for fifty hogsheads of tobacco weighing 64,166 pounds gross, probably not over 52,000 pounds net, every hogshead numbered, for which he brought in returns a draft on a Nashville bank for $1,000, two hundred pairs of boots, $800, and $211 in sugar and coffee. This was probably after paying freight charges, about three cents per pound, for the tobacco. About this time two steamboats, the General Green and the General Robertson, entered the Cumberland River, driving most of the flatboats men out of the business, having a monopoly of the shipping trade up to 1822, making Clarksville the principal shipping point, which was then a town of only forty families — 215 white population, and a number of Negroes.

The want of some satisfactory explanation, or the failure of all investigations to throw light on the witch mystery, gave rise to a speculative idea that John and Drew Bell had learned ventriloquism and some subtle art while on these trips to New Orleans, and taught the same to their young sister Betsy, for the purpose of attracting people and making money. This conjecture was widely circulated, and checked many people in their purpose of visiting the scene of the excitement. Notwithstanding this explanation was accepted by many, it was the silliest of all solutions attempted. If the parties were able to perform such wonders, they only had to make the fact known to have reaped a fortune. But to the contrary, they tried to keep it a secret, and when known it brought both suffering and loss to the family. Moreover, John Bell, Jr., was absent, visiting relatives in North Carolina, six months or more during the height of the excitement, and he could not possibly have had anything to do with it. Drew was also absent at times, and still no difference was observed in the manifestations when they were both absent or present. The witch entertained visitors in the reception room just the same when Betsy was present or retired to her own chamber. There was also knocking on the doors and outer walls, and rattling on the house-top heard, when every member of the family were known to be within. And as soon as the family and visitors retired for sleep, every room full, doors and windows securely closed, the cover was stripped from every bed and pillows and sheets jerked from under strong men. If the Bell brothers and sister, had been capable of making such demonstrations, could they have continued the exhibitions so long undiscovered by the shrewd detectives who were constantly on the alert? Or would they have heartlessly inflicted so much distress upon their father and family? No one in that community, familiar with the facts and demonstrations, knowing the affections of the children for their parents, and devotion to each other, ever believed it. They knew it was impossible. Betsy was not only frightened, but was severely punished in so many ways that she cheerfully submitted to any and every investigation proposed, even to the ridiculous treatment of cranks, conjurers, and witch doctors, in the hope of relief from some source. Drewry Bell never married. He lived quite a secluded bachelor's life, accumulating considerable property. He died at his home in that vicinity January 1st, 1865. It is said by neighbors that he lived under forebodings and dreadful, apprehension that the witch would visit some calamity on him. He charged every strange noise and occurrence to the haunt, reciting mysterious occurrences to his friends, believing that the spirit was ever present about his premises, and through fear he kept some man employed on the place to keep him company.

Richard Williams Bell settled on his portion of the land inherited from his father's estate, buying other interests, and devoted himself to agriculture. He was endowed with a strong intellect, and was the most cultured of the family, noted for his splendid business qualifications and frugality, and especially was he distinguished for his integrity of character, his deep piety and devotion to his religious principles, his tender nature, and promptness in lending a helping hand where help was needed, he was one of nature's noblemen — a good man and valuable citizen. He had not an enemy in the broad land. His neighbors trusted him implicitly, and relied upon him as a true friend and safe counselor in all things, and his name is cherished to this day by all who knew him.

Williams Bell was a boy at the time of the witch affliction, which the Bell's have always alluded to as "our family trouble," but he was old enough, and probably just the right age, to receive a deep and lasting impression of what occurred, what he saw, felt and heard, things that were well calculated to impress a boy's mind. He waited upon his father during the last year of his life, and when able to go out, accompanied him wherever he went about the farm or in the neighborhood, witnessed his contortions and excruciating sufferings, and heard the derisive songs and fearful anathemas pronounced against him by the witch — terrifying invectives that were calculated to appall the stoutest heart and leave an impress seared as by fire. The imprint was never erased, and every recurring thought of the dire events came like a convulsing nightmare. After mature years he consulted with his brothers and sister Betsy, comparing their recollections with the notes of his own memory, from which he wrote the thrilling details of "Our Family Trouble," and no reader who ever knew the writer will question the truth of a single word of it, no matter what may be their faith or opinion concerning the mystery, or their views about witch craft of olden times. Williams Bell died October 24th, 1857, at the age of forty-six years, just in the prime of life and his greatest usefulness. He left a good estate for his widow and children. He was three times married, his first wife being Sallie Gunn, daughter of Rev. Thomas Gunn; second marriage with Susan Gunn, daughter of Rev. James Gunn, and third wife, Eliza Orndorff. James Allen Bell was the eldest son by his first wife. He received careful training at the hands of his father, and developed steady business habits and strong convictions, attaining to prominence quite early in life, taking a leading place in politics and public affairs, and about 1870 was nominated by the County Democratic Convention and elected by the people to represent the county in the State Legislature. At the close of the term he sold his farm and other interests in Robertson County and moved to Adairville, Ky., engaging in the tobacco business, where he still resides, and is highly esteemed by the people of both Logan and Robertson counties. He married Miss Eugenia Chambers, a lady of many personal charms and accomplishments. They have raised three children, a son and two daughters, of whom they have just cause to feel proud. Williams Bell's youngest son, Ninyon Oliver, by his last marriage, is a substantial farmer and owns a fine home adjoining the old Bell place in fact his farm includes the old residence site and surroundings.

Joel E. Bell was the youngest child of John and Lucy Bell. The writer enjoyed a personal acquaintance with him for twenty-five years, and learned to appreciate his warm and generous friendship. He was a man of noble impulse, clear practicable head and settled convictions, favored by an indomitable spirit full of fiery enthusiasm, and always left a strong and pleasing impress on those with whom he came in contact. He took a leading part in all matters looking to the advancement of the public welfare, and his zeal for the accomplishment of whatever he undertook knew no bounds.

He was a strong Baptist, a religious enthusiast, always overflowing with the love of God, and his last days were spent in zealous work for the Master's cause. He attended the associational meetings, delivered happy little speeches pregnant with practical ideas, infusing spirit in the members, giving freely of his own means for the advancement of religious enterprises. There are but few Baptist ministers and prominent laymen in Tennessee and Southern Kentucky Who do not remember old Brother Bell with tender emotions. He died in 1890 at the age of seventy-seven years, ripe for the enjoyment of that sweet repose which remains for the righteous. Joel Bell sold his farm in the west end of the county, the place now occupied by Lee Smith, about 1855, and moved to a large brick dwelling at the cross roads four miles north of Springfield — the Adairville road — where he died. He was twice married, and was fortunate in both matches.

# Chapter 4

## *Betsy Bell and Her Trials*

Elizabeth, the youngest daughter of John and Lucy Bell, was born in 1805, and was only twelve years of age when "our family troubles" commenced — a light, hearted, romping lass whose roguish beauty and mischievous glance made the hearts of the boys go pit pat, while she yet enjoyed most the gay notes of the woodland songsters, or a stroll with her associates in search of wild flowers, berries, etc., along the riverside where the murmuring waves lent an enchantment to the pursuit. Betsy, however, developed rapidly, and at the age of fifteen had ripened into lovely young womanhood, and was noted for her extraordinary beauty and winsome ways. She was a blonde, symmetrical in form, presenting a charming figure of uncommon grace, with a fine suit of soft silky hair, which hung in beautiful waves, in contrast with her fair complexion, and with all, there was enchantment in the mischievous twinkle of her large deeply set blue eyes. She was also characterized for her keen wit and sparkling humor; nor had her domestic education, that which added most to a young girl's popularity in olden times, been neglected, to all of which must be added industrious habits, gentleness and womanly dignity. It is no wonder that she was the pet of the family and the favorite in society, nor is it surprising that young Joshua Gardner should have lost both his head and heart in admiration for the fair beauty in whom the observing bachelor school master discovered so many charms. Gardner had now become very earnest in his devotions, and was never more happy than when in her society. And it was said that the sentiment was reciprocated, he being the first young man to impress her with his attentions. In fact their fondness for each others society became the subject of general remark among the young people. They were regarded as lovers, and Joshua was the recipient of many congratulations on his good fortune in winning the affections of the fairest beauty in the land. The affiance was marked by a passionate tenderness and adoration which neither could well conceal, and it was given still more notoriety by the witch, whose keen observations and cutting remarks frequently drove them from the presence of other company, for a walk in the lawn or seats under the favorite pear tree. However, it was the manner in which Kate appeared that caused serious forebodings. It was a soft melancholy voice, sighing in the distance and gradually approaching nearer with gentle pleadings in loud whispers, "Please Betsy Bell, don't have Joshua Gardner. Please Betsy Bell, don't marry Joshua Gardner." Over and over was this entreaty earnestly repeated by the mysterious voice in the most beseeching and supplicating tones, so doleful and disconsolate that it caused a shudder to creep over everyone who heard it. It was so intensely persuasive, gentle and sweet, so extremely mystifying, that it not only bewildered the lovers, but brought perplexity and confusion into every social, circle where the matter was discussed as the most absorbing theme. Why should Betsy Bell not wed Joshua Gardner? He was handsome and gracious, well educated, intelligent and entertaining, high spirited, industrious and energetic, and noted for his strict moral character and pleasing deportment; he was highly connected and possessed sufficient means for a good start in life. His integrity was above reproach, and he stood before the community as a model young man. Then why this dismal foreboding of the witch? Why should Betsy Bell spurn his manly devotions? No one could surmise or conjecture a single reason, and all hearts warmed in deep sympathy for their betrothment. [sic] Betsy had suffered extreme torture, the anguish of terror by contact with the frightful ghost, and was deeply impressed with the witch's earnest solicitude as a premonition of some dire consequence. Joshua, however, was stouter of heart. The burning passion which thrilled his soul was like a consuming flame, and grew stronger as the persecutions increased. He had his own opinions and conjectures about the mystery, and though he could not solve it, he was willing to brook all danger of the witch's power to visit distress or greater evil than had already been inflicted, and he was ready to endure all for the sake of her whom he loved so tenderly, madly. He was assured that Betsy loved him as passionately in return. Hers was a stronger, a more rational devotion, looking also to the future, weighing deliberately the consequences that might result from a mistake, and thought it best to prolong the engagement and await further developments, hoping that the mystery might be solved or the witch would disappear, leaving them in the full enjoyment of each other's love and all of their sweet anticipations of uninterrupted happiness. This was the agreement, and there was no abatement in their devotions; the attachment grew stronger and the ties more tender and passionate. Betsy was not without friends, sympathy and consolation all through this long and trying ordeal. Her parents were deeply sensible of her sufferings and the cloud of sorrow that overshadowed her, threatening to crush the spirit and hope of her young life, and did all that was in their power to alleviate her distress. Her mother, Mrs. Lucy Bell, whose influence was the controlling power, and swayed like magic in molding and shaping the character of her children, was watchful of her every want and care. The brothers were not negligent in. providing diversions for her relaxation. Theny Thorn and Becky Porter never deserted her in moments when courage was needed to withstand the dreadful scenes that were enacted. They witnessed the fearful convulsions of hysteria which so frequently came on suddenly, with the announcement of Kate's presence, suppressing her breath until life was almost extinct. They had heard her frantic screams from violent pain, complaining that the "old thing" was sticking pins in her body. They had heard the sound of the blow, and saw the tinge left by the invisible hand that slapped her cheeks. They had seen her tucking comb snatched by magic from her head and slammed on the floor, her beautiful hair disheveled and all tangled in an instant, and heard Kate's hilarious laughter enjoying the freak. They had witnessed her shoes coming unlaced and slipping from her feet at the witch's suggestion, and observed many other terrifying and tormenting acts, accompanied with vile threats, while watching with Betsy night after night, gossiping with the witch that she might have some rest. But few girls could be persuaded to withstand such frightful scenes under apprehensions of greater calamity, but timid as they were their sympathy and devotion made them strong; courageous to endure and suffer with their friend in any misfortune that might come. Their presence and sympathy encouraged Betsy to bear her persecutions, and hold out bravely in the hope that the mystery would soon be dispelled. James Long and Alex Gooch were frequently around contributing to some diversion, and Joshua Gardner continued his rapturous attentions, foregoing every desire of his own heart for her pleasure and comfort. Prof. Richard Powell had ended his career as a pedagogue and was not so much about the Bell home. He had entered the political arena and become a leading politician and foremost in all public affairs. He was several times elected to the State Legislature, where he distinguished himself as a lawmaker of ability and gained wide popularity.

# Chapter 5

## *The Homestead — Graveyard — Witch Stories and Surroundings*

The old Bell farm is about one mile from Adams Station, a village that sprang into existence in 1859-60, during the building of the Edgefield and Kentucky Railroad, which is now the Southeastern branch of the Louisville and Nashville system. It lies on the south side of Red River, bordering some distance on that pretty stream, stretching back nearly one mile over a beautiful fertile valley. The greater portion of the farm was cleared by John Bell during the first twenty years of the present century. Here Dean, the faithful Negro who proudly mastered the big wagon and team in the train from the old North State, that landed the family safely, deserves honorable mention. He was noted for being the best axe man and rail splitter that ever entered the forest of this country. He was small in statue, but powerfully muscled, and no two men were ever found who could match him in felling timber, he taking one side of a tree, against two men on the opposite, and invariably cutting the deepest kerf; and so with the mall and wedge, he could beat any two of the best rail splitters in the country. Dean was as proud of this distinction as ever John Sullivan was of his pugilistic championship, and he was indeed a valuable man in the forest at that time, as he was faithful and useful every way, and Mr. Bell thought a great deal of him and treated him kindly, as he did all of his Negroes, but money could not buy Dean. Red River is a bold strong stream, with some interesting scenery, and bubbling springs bursting out along its banks. During the early settlement the stream abounded with game and fish, furnishing much sport for the natives, and young people frequently gathered at favorite places for picnics and fishing frolics. The noted spring mentioned by Willams Bell in this sketch, designated by the witch as the hiding place of a large sum of money, breaks out on the southeast corner of the place, near the river, from which flows the bubbling waters of lethe.

The residence was a double log house, one and a half stories high, a wide passage or hallway between, and an ell-room with passage, the building weather-boarded on the outside, furnishing six large comfortable rooms and two halls, and was one of the best residences in the country at that time. It was located on a slight elevation in the plane, nearly a half-mile back from the river, a large orchard in the rear, and the lawn well set in pear trees. The farm has been divided and the old buildings were long since torn away and the logs used for building cabins, still standing on the Joel Bell place, now owned by Lee Smith. No one cared to occupy the premises after the death of Mrs. Lucy Bell, when it was vacated, and for some time used for storing grain. The only sign now remaining is a few scattered stones from the foundation, and three of the old pear trees that surrounded the house, planted about the time or before John Bell bought the place, some ninety years ago. One of these trees measures nearly seven feet around the trunk; it, however, shows signs of rapid decay. The public highway, known as the Brown's Ford and Spring field road, ran through the place within one hundred yards of the house, and it was no uncommon thing during the witch excitement to find a horse hitched to every fence corner of the long lane, by people calling to hear the witch talk and investigate the sensation. Many stories were told regarding spectres and apparitions of various kinds seen, and uncommon sounds heard along this 1ane — strange lights and jack-o-lanterns flitting across the field. There is nothing, how ever, authentic in reference to these things except the incident told by Dr. Gooch, who saw the old house enveloped in flames, and the musical feast at the spring, related by Gunn and Bartlett. There were many superstitious people in the country who believed the witch was a reality, something supernatural, beyond human power or comprehension, which had been clearly demonstrated. This is the way many reasoned about the mystery. Kate arrogantly claimed to be all things, possessing the power to assume any shape, form or character, that of human, beast, varmint, fowl or fish, and circumstances went to confirm the assertion. Therefore people with vivid imaginations were capable of seeing many strange sights and things that could not be readily accounted for, which were credited to the witch. Kate was a great scapegoat. The goblin's favorite form, however, was that of a rabbit, and this much is verified beyond question, the hare ghost took malicious pleasure in hopping out into the road, showing itself to everyone who ever passed through that lane. This same rabbit is there plentifully to this day, and can't be exterminated. Very few men know a witch rabbit; only experts can distinguish one from the ordinary molly cottontail. The experts in that section, however, are numerous, and no one to this good day will eat a rabbit that has a black spot on the bottom of its left hind foot. When the spot is found, the foot is carefully cut off and placed in the hip pocket, and the body buried on the north side of an old log.

Some of these people believed the spook escaped from an

Indian grave on the Bell place, by the reckless disinterment of the red man's bones, but Kate's own statement, which was afterwards contradicted, is the only shadow of evidence found to sustain this opinion.

The Bell graveyard is located on a gravelly knoll about three hundred yards north of the side of the old dwelling, where repose the dust of John Bell, Sr., his wife Lucy, and sons Benjamin, Zadok, and Richard Williams, the last named who tells the story of "Our Family Trouble." A beautiful grove of cedar and walnut trees surround the sacred spot, keeping silent watch over the graves of loved ones whose bodies rest there. Wild grape vines, supported by large trunks, spread their far-reaching tendrils over every branch and twig of the trees, forming a delightful alcove. Native strawberries grow all about, and wild flowers of many varieties blossom in their season, filling nature's bower with grateful fragrance, and decorating the graves in living beauty. It is here that the wild wood songsters gather to chant their sweetest lays, and the timid hare finds retreat and hiding from the prowling huntsman. Sweet solemnity hovers over the scene like the morning halo mantling the orb of light in gorgeous beauty.

There are numbers of unregenerate men who can perhaps muster sufficient courage to pass a city of towering shafts and monuments, but can: not be induced to approach near so sacred a spot as this after the sun has hidden his face behind the shadow of night. It presents nothing fanciful, or inviting to their view, but rather a scene of the ideal home of weird spirits. But to people who trust Providence, admire tile beauties of nature, and fear not devils, this bowery alcove of woodland trees, evergreens, vines and flowers, sheltering sacred dust, appears one of the most lovely and majestic spots on earth.

Let those who feel the need of it, have magnificent stately monuments and lofty shafts mounted with a dove, or a pinnacle finger pointing heavenward, but give me such a paradise of living green as this, planted and nurtured by the hand of the All Wise Creator, where angels may delight to meet and commune, breathing sweet incense distilled by the zephyrs from nature's own flowers, keeping vigilance until the last trump shall sound, and why should I care for a granite shaft reaching to the skies, or grumble at a poor scrawny spook for wanting to hide beneath its cover, to catch a pure breath while hazing around to avoid Satan?

On the opposite side of the river from the Bell place, is the William La Prade farm, now owned by M. L. Killebrew, and just below Killebrew's, all between the river and Elk Fork Creek, is the

Fort settlement, a large and influential family, distinguished among the pioneers, and whose descendants still maintain the honored name. On the east was located the Gunns and Johnsons, all having good farms. James Johnson and two sons, John and Calvin, were Bell's nearest neighbors, and next the Gunn families. James Johnson was a grand old man. He was the founder of Johnson's Camp Ground on his place, which was kept up by his sons, the Gunns and other good people, long years after his death, as late as 1854. Great crowds of people from a circle of twenty or thirty miles, gathered there annually, spending weeks in a season of religious enjoyment. Many descendants of these excellent families — Gunns and Johnsons — make up the present citizenship maintaining as a precious heritage the good names left to them. Also the Goochs, Longs, Porters, Jerry Batts, Miles, Byrns, Bartlett, Ruffin, and other good names among the early settlers, are still well represented.

One mile above Bell's the Clark brothers had a mill to which the early settlers carried their grain and grist. Later, Fort's mill was built below, and several other mills erected on Elk Fork. Morris & Merritt bought out the Clarks and converted the old mill into a cotton ginning, thread spinning and wool carding factory. It was said that the witch took up at this factory after seven years absence and return. The manager told the story to customers, that frequently after shutting down the mill, the operators would hardly reach home before the machinery would be heard apparently in full movement, and returning hastily, opening the door, he would find everything perfectly still as he had left it. There is, however, no evidence to be had now verifying the statement.

# Chapter 6

## *Mrs. Kate Batts and the Witch*

It is proper that the reader should, before perusing "Our Family Trouble" and other accounts of the witch, be introduced to Mrs. Kate Batts, who was a noted lady in that community, remarkable for her eccentricities, who survived long after John Bell and is well remembered by many citizens still living. There were two Batts families, who were in no way related. Jerry Batts was a very prominent man, and his descendants make up part of the present good citizenship of that community.

Frederick Batts and wife Kate had three children, Jack, Calvin and Mary. They had no relatives and lived very much unto themselves. Their children died in advance of the turn of life and the family has become extinct. The boys were all, spindling and gawky, and very droll, and did not take in society. Mary, however, was a beautiful bright girl and very popular. Frederick Batts was an invalid, a helpless cripple, the greater part of his life, and his wife Kate assumed control of the farm, the family and all business affairs, and was successful in accumulating by her management, keeping the one idea of money making before her. They were well to do people, owned a very good farm, a number of Negroes, and were forehanded, having always some money to lend. Nothing of a disreputable nature attached to the family character. They were respectable people, except for Mrs. Batts' eccentricity, which made many hold the family at as great a distance as possible. She was a large fleshy woman, weighing over two hundred pounds, and was headstrong and very exacting in her dealings with men. She was exceedingly jealous of her rights, not always knowing what they were, conceiving the idea that everybody was trying to beat her out of something. Her tongue was fearful. She did not hesitate to tackle any man who came under the ban of her displeasure, with a scourge of epithets. This, however, was tolerated as a weakness, and excited the sympathy of the better class, who humored her whims, but no one cared to encounter her organ of articulation when she was in a bad humor, and especially the ladies, who were generally afraid of her, and could not endure her methods and dominating spirit. The superstitious believed that she was a witch, and this conjecture was strengthened by her habit of begging a brass pin from every woman she met, which trifle was supposed to give her power over the donor, and some ladies were careful to put their pins far away when "Old Kate" came in sight. Notwithstanding Mrs. Batts was around every few days, traveling her circuit once a week, trading and gossiping, the superstitious were careful to keep their apprehensions concealed from her. They were all smiles and joy, and spared no opportunity to make "Aunt Kate" happy in everything but one — and were exceedingly regretful that there was not a pin on the place.

Mrs. Batts kept her Negro women employed mostly at spinning, weaving cotton, flax and wool, making jeans, linsey, linen, etc., and knitting stockings after night until late bed time, and always had something to sell, and would buy all the surplus wool rolls and other raw material wanted in her business, and this furnished her an excuse for visiting regularly over the neighborhood. Mrs. Batts was very aristocratic in her own conceit, believing that her property entitled her to move in the highest circle of society, and she put on extraordinary airs and used high sounding bombastic words, assimilating, as she thought, aristocracy, which subjected her to much ridicule and made her the laughing stock of the community. Moreover, she was anxious to give her timid boy, Calvin, a matrimonial boost, and never hesitated to invade the society of young people, who were amused by her quaint remarks. The girls, however, dreaded her presence in mixed company, lest she should unwittingly say something to cause a blush. However she never neglected to put in a word for her noble boy, who resembled a bean pole. "Girls, keep your eyes on Calvin; he's all warp and no filling, but he'll weave a yard wide" — referring to her own large proportions.

Mrs. Batts kept an old gray horse expressly for the saddle. Old Gray was saddled every morning as regular as the sun shone, though Aunt Kate was never known to ride. She invariably walked, carrying a copperas riding skirt on her left arm, two little Negro boys walking by her side, and Phillis, her waiting maid, in front leading the old gray horse. This caravan was known as "Kate Batts' troop." No difference where she went, if entering the finest parlor in the country, Aunt Kate would habitually spread the copperas skirt over the seat offered her, and set on it. With all of these peculiarities and eccentricities, "Sister Kate" was an enthusiastic Christian, always expatiating on the Scripture and the goodness of God, and would have her share of rejoicing in every meeting, and it never required an excess of spiritual animation to warm her up to business. She was a member of Red River Church and a regular attendant, always late, but in time to get happy before the meeting closed.

On one occasion, Rev. Thomas Felts was conducting a revival

meeting, which had been in progress several days, and a deep religious feeling had been awakened, the house being crowded every day with anxious people. Just as Parson Felts had concluded a rousing sermon awakening sinners to repentance, and called the mourners to the front, and the whole audience engaged in singing rapturous praise and transporting melody, the Batts' troop arrived. Phillis observed "Old Missus" had already caught the spirit and was filling up on glory, hurriedly hitched Old Gray and made a rush for the house. The meeting had reached its highest tension, the house was packed, and the congregation on foot singing with the spirit. The interest centered around Joe Edwards, who was down on his all fours at the mourner's bench, supplicating and praying manfully. Joe Edwards was a good citizen, but a desperately wicked and undone sinner, and everybody was anxious to have him converted. Especially were his religious friends in deep sympathy, sharing the burden of sorrow he was trying to throw off, as he seemed to be almost at the point of trusting, and the brethren had gathered around, instructing and urging him on. Just at this critical moment Sister Batts rushed in, and elbowing her way into the circle, she deliberately spread her copperas riding skirt all over Joe Edwards and sat down on him. The poor man did not know what had happened; he felt that he was in the throes of the last desperate struggle with Satan and that the devil was on top. He shouted and yelled the louder, "Oh I am sinking, sinking. Oh take my burden Jesus and make the devil turn me loose or I will go down, down, and be lost forever in torment. Oh save me, save me, blessed Lord."

A good brother invited Sister Batts to another seat, but she politely declined with a flourish of big words, as was her custom when putting on dignified airs. "No I thank you; this is so consoling to my disposition that I feel amply corrugated."

"But," insisted the good deacon, "you are crowding the mourner."

"Oh that don't disburse my perspicuity; I'm a very plain woman and do love to homigate near the altar whar th'r Lord am making confugation among th'r sinners."

"But, Sister Batts, the man is suffocating," still interposed the deacon. "Yes, bless Jesus, let him suffocate; he's getting closer to th'r Lord," exclaimed Sister Batts.

The situation had now become serious. The whole house had caught on, and was bursting with tittering laughter. Sister Batts felt the foundation beneath her giving away, and was caught by two brethren just as she threw up her hands, in time to prevent a still more ludicrous scene. Joe Edwards rose up shouting joyously for his deliverance, as if some unknown spirit had snatched him from the vasty deep. Sister Batts clasped her hands and shouted, "Bless th'r Lord, bless my soul, Jesus am so good to devolve His poor critters from the consternation of Satan's mighty dexterity." The affair had reached such a comical and extremely ludicrous stage, that the audience could no longer restrain its resistibility to a simper, and many left the house hurriedly for au outdoor open air free laugh. This ended the service, breaking up the meeting. The preacher could do nothing but dismiss the remainder of the congregation, who were suffering from a suppressed tittering sensation, holding their sides out of respect for the minister and religion.

Phillis was a strong believer in "Ole Missus." Describing the incident she said: "I neber seed Satan whipped outen er meetin so quick in all'er my bawn days. Sooner an Ole Missus sot down on dat man, de devil tuck out under der flo an' de man hollered glory, glory, lemme up, lemme up. Ole Miss paid no 'tention tu enybody. She sat dar, an' 'menced gittin happy herself, an' all de folks in de house 'menced shoutin'. De man he got so full of glory he ware gwinter git up anyhow an' 'menced drawing hiz hine legs up sorter like er cow, an' den drapped back, case Ole Miss ware still dar, an' she want'er gwineter git up tell ole Satan wuz mashed clean outen him. Hit made Mister Joe Edwards sweat like er hoss, but he am got mighty good 'ligion now, dat will last him tell der next meetin."


As soon as the loquacious visitor developed the propensity for articulation, people became importunate in their entreaties, begging the mysterious voice to disclose its character, nature, who or what it was, and what its mission, to which importunities various answers were given, but no explanation that seemed to satisfy the anxious curiosity. Finally Rev. James Gunn undertook in a conversation with the gnome to draw out the information. The goblin declared that it could not trifle with a preacher or tell Brother Gunn a lie, and if he must know the truth, it was nothing more nor less than old Kate Batts' witch, and was determined to haunt and torment old Jack Bell as long as he lived. This announcement seemed to fit the case precisely and satisfy a certain element to a fraction. Less superstitious and more considerate persons did not expect the witch to divulge the truth, and of course did not believe a word concerning Mrs. Batts' agency in the matter; that was impossible. But the explanation pleased those, who wanted it so. It served for a brand new and most startling sensation in the mysterious developments, and all tongues were set to wagging. Men and women looked aghast,

# Chapter 7

## *Witchcraft of the Bible: Opinions of Rev. John Wesley, Dr. Clark, and other Distinguished Divines and Commentators*

The writer has no theory to present regarding the Bell Witch phenomena, nor has he any opinion to advance concerning witchcraft, sorcery, spiritualism or psychology in any form, but prefers quoting from Scripture, and the reasoning of distinguished men, learned in theology, and experienced in psychical research. He frankly confesses his ignorance of such matters, and the total lack of both inclination and ability to enter into the investigation of the fathomless subject. Having known the history of the Bell Witch from a boy's earliest recollections, and now having collected and compiled the testimony, he is convinced by the overwhelming evidence, that the circumstances detailed by Williams Bell, and supported by others, as unreasonable as they may appear, are literally true — such things did happen, but no further can we venture.

Knowing the character of the men and women who testify to these things, no one can disbelieve them, or believe that they would have willfully misrepresented the facts; nor can it reasonably be said that so many reputable witnesses had fallen into an abnormal state of mind, and were so easily deceived in all of their rigid investigations. A man may be arraigned for trial on the charge of murder, the court and jury knowing nothing about the facts and circumstances, but they are bound by both physical and moral law to believe and find the man guilty on the testimony of reputable witnesses, detailing the facts and circumstances, and yet may form no opinion or idea as to the state of mind or cause that prompted the prisoner to commit the murder. So it is in this instance; the testimony is convincing of the truth of the wonderful phenomena, at John Bell's, but the motive or cause is beyond our comprehension, and to this extent the facts must be accepted. It would be a shameful display of one's ignorance to deny on general principles the existence of the thing or fact, in the face of such evidence, because he did not witness it, and cannot comprehend it. Might as well the jury, after hearing the evidence, discharge the prisoner on the grounds that they did not see the act committed, and could not believe the man guilty of a deed so atrocious.

The writer, however, wishes to present every phase of the Bell Witch phenomena, together with some quotations from the Bible on which many people in all ages have based their superstition; also the reasoning of some spiritually enlightened and successful ministers of Christ's doctrine, and opinions on ancient witchcraft as presented by the Bible, together with the ideas of modern spiritualism, for the benefit of those who are dis posed to investigate. Christianity of the present day has generally abandoned the doctrine of "ministering spirits" as a faith leading up to a danger line where there can be no distinction between that and modern spiritualism. Dr. Bond, a distinguished Methodist divine and editor, who has most forcibly combated the faith on the grounds that, that which cannot be explained is not to be believed, and for the best reason that many deeply pious minds have become involved in confusion and error in trying to exercise this discriminating faith, and he argues that all premonitions, omens and spectral appearances are a common phenomena of disordered senses, and that the doctrine of the spirit world is unscriptural and dangerous in the extreme, and that theologians have no right to say that the spirits of the dead live about us, and commune with us, and minister to us.

Notwithstanding all such arguments and the efforts to put away superstition, to ridicule and laugh it out of existence, there is scarcely any one who is free from every form of superstition. Certainly the Christian world gets its superstition from the Bible, if it is not innate, and it is very hard to discard, and still accept all other things that the Book teaches as divine revelation. There are but few people, however, who are willing to admit their superstition, lest they be laughed at and characterized as weak-minded, crazy, etc. Even Dr. Clark, the great John Wesley, the founder of Methodism, and many other distinguished writers and commentators, have not escaped this criticism. Mr. Wesley, however, was bold in speaking his sentiments and rather boasted of his belief in witchcraft. He wrote and spoke about the Epworth ghost that haunted the family some thirty years.

Rev. L. Tyerman, in his *Life and Times of Wesley*, says Wesley has been censured and ridiculed for this credulity. Did Wesley deserve this? The reader must not forget the undeniable, though mysterious, supernatural noises in .the Epworth rectory. He must also bear in mind that one of the most striking features in Wesley's religious character was his deep rooted, intense, powerful and impelling convictions of the dread realities of an unseen world. This great conviction took possession of the man, he loved it, cherished it, tried to instill it into all of his helpers, all of his people, and without it he would never have undertaken the Herculean labor, and endured the almost unparalleled opprobrium that he did. Besides his own justification of himself is more easily sneered at than answered.

He (Wesley) writes:

"With my last breath, will I bear my testimony against giving up to infidels one great proof of the invisible world; I mean, that of witchcraft and apparitions, confirmed by the testimony of all ages. The English in general, and indeed, most of the men of learning in Europe, have given up all accounts of witches and apparitions as mere old wives' fables. I am sorry for it, and I willingly take this opportunity of entering my solemn protest against this violent compliment, which so many that believe the Bible pay to those who do not believe it. I owe them no such service. I take knowledge these are at the bottom of the out cry which has been raised, and with such insolence spread throughout the nation in direct opposition not only to the Bible, but to the suffrage of the wisest and best of men in all ages and nations. They well know (whether Christians know or not) that the giving up of Witchcraft is in effect giving up the Bible; and they know, on the other hand, that if but one account of the intercourse of men with separate spirits be admitted their whole castle in the air: deism, atheism, materialism — falls to the ground. I know no reason, therefore, why we should suffer even this weapon to be wrested out of our hands. Indeed, there are numerous arguments besides this, which abundantly confute their vain imaginations. But we need not be hooted out of one; neither reason nor religion requires this. One of the capital objections to all of these accounts is, 'Did you ever see an apparition yourself?' No, nor did I ever see a murder; yet I believe there is such a thing. The testimony of unexceptionable witnesses fully convince me both of the one and the other."

Was Mr. Wesley right or not? John Wesley was perhaps the greatest evangelist the world has produced since the days of Paul, and now after more than one hundred years can we, judging from his wonderful work, deny that the spirit of God, and even ministering angels as he claimed, attended him in his mighty spread of the gospel? Was any living man ever endowed with such a wonderful capacity for traveling, preaching and writing, under so many hardships and privations? And does it not appear that he was inspired and guided by the same power that sup ported Paul? The infidel may find some way of denying this, but the Christian believer, hardly. Then to deny Wesley's teachings respecting Bible authority for witchcraft; or charge his faith to a disordered mind, is to accuse God with raising up a great man to propagate a monstrous error, and furthermore is to discard the hundreds of passages all through the Bible from Genesis to Revelations, and agree with infidelity that all such Scripture is false, and that being false, there can be nothing reliable in God's Word. For illustration take the case of the witch of Endor, whom Saul approached in disguise after night, because he had ordered all witches and wizards put to death, and the witch of Endor was shy of violating the order. Now God had withdrawn from Saul and answered him no more, and he sought a familiar spirit, promising the woman that no harm should come to her for this thing. I. Samuel xxviii, 3: Now Samuel was dead and all Israel had lamented him, and buried him. Then said the woman, Whom shall I bring up unto thee? And he said, Bring me up Samuel. And when the woman saw Samuel, Saul asked what form is he of? And she said, An old man cometh tip, and he is covered with a mantle. And Saul perceived that it was Samuel, and he stooped with his face to the ground, and bowed himself. And Samuel said to Saul, Why hast thou disquieted me, to bring me up?

Read the whole chapter — Saul's trouble and Samuel's prophecy of what was to occur tomorrow, etc. There can be no doubt that this was the identical Samuel who had anointed Saul King of Israel, if the Bible be true; moreover the witch did not know Saul until after Samuel appeared. This cannot be placed in the catalogue of God's miracles, because it was the woman's profession; and she is supposed to have brought up bad, as well as good spirits, and she was popularly known in the country as a witch possessing this power, and therefore Saul was directed to go to her. If this be a miracle, then God used witches and wizards to perform miracles, and Paul and others who cast out devils in the name of Christ, were wizards or seers. How will Christian people who deny Mr. Wesley's position reconcile this question? Furthermore, additional light on this subject will be found in I. Chronicles xiii. Saul died for asking counsel of one that had a familiar spirit, to inquire of it. Evidently God did not approve of the works of this woman, though He permitted such works. And why? Because it is in accord with the philosophy of creation of worlds, the reign of devils on earth, and designs of the Almighty in the scheme of redemption, answers the believers in a spiritual world. They hold from the teachings of such Scripture, that there is a spiritual world, just as this is a natural or material world. They hold that the inner man, or life, is a refined substance, which, when separated from the natural body by death, passes into the spiritual world as tangible to those in the spiritual world as the body is to the material world. Also that bad as well as good spirits enter this spiritual kingdom, and that there is a continual struggle between the good and bad in that world as in this. They believe that the spiritual body is a very refined substance, like electricity, and that matter is no obstruction to it, that it may and does have communion with the spirit in the body, knows every thought and action of the human mind, our wants and necessities, and therefore departed spirits become ministering angels or spirits to friends in this world, and just in proportion as man lives in nearness to God, spiritually, rising high in the scale of mental, and heartfelt devotion, developing his spiritual nature — that refined substance called animal electricity or magnetism, which is the spirit — so much more is he capable of recognizing the presence of ministering spirits by communication or even by spiritual sight; and that it is through this medium that people see apparitions, receive premonitions and warnings of what is to occur. These believers hold that the visitation of angels so often recorded in both the Old and New Testaments, were simply ministering spirits, sometimes referred to as angels, and often, as "man" or "men" and spirits. As in the case of Paul, Acts xvi. 9: when "a man" appeared to Paul in the night, "There stood a man of Macedonia, and prayed him, saying: Come over into Macedonia and help us." Now the question, who was this "man?" Was he a spirit, a Macedonian? In Rev. xxii. the angel appearing to John, tells him that he was one of the prophets. The Psalmist says, "The angels of the Lord encamped around them, and delivereth them." And again, "He shall give his angels charge over thee to keep thee in all thy ways." The Apostle Paul says, speaking of angelic spirits "Are they not ministering spirits, sent forth to minister to them who shall be heirs of salvation?" So it is believed from these and many other such expressions in the Bible, that the atmosphere possesses the property of telegraphing that is yet to be developed and better understood, by which the spiritual world is in constant communication with this, and that spirits travel like thought or the electric flash, throughout all space in an instant, and space is annihilated. It is, therefore, believed that the principles of the moral government of God are the same under every dispensation, that this could not be. changed in the very nature of God's creation, and that the ministry of angels and exemplified under every dispensation, showing the uniformity of God's works and government.

The question is asked: Are angels not men, spirits that once dwelt in the body on earth? Who was "the man Gabriel" that spoke to Daniel of the four great monarchies? Who was the prophet that talked to John on the isle of Patmos? Who was the "young man" that stood in the sepulcher, clothed in a long white garment. Who were the "two men" that stood by them at the sepulcher in shining garments, telling the disciples that "He is not here but is risen," as recorded by Luke xxiv? Who were the "two men" that spoke to the men of Galilee when Jesus ascended from Mount Olivet? — Acts i., 9-11. This faith must be the most comforting thing on earth to the soul that can exercise it discriminately. But the danger is in going too far, losing sight of God, and relying on ministering spirits, for there may be evil as well as good spirits, and how can one know whether the manifestation is from Christ's Kingdom, or that of outer darkness? God showed His disapproval of Saul's act in calling up so good a spirit as Samuel through a witch medium, knowing that the Lord had withdrawn from him on account of his wickedness and disobedience; yet the witch was gifted with that power — perhaps just as the present day mediums have developed electrical force.

However, Mr. Wesley was not alone in pro claiming this belief in a spiritual kingdom and ministering spirits. Many learned theologians support this doctrine. Dr. Adam Clarke, the great scholar and commentator, in his Commentary, vol. xi., page 299, says: "I believe there is a supernatural and spiritual world in which human spirits, both good and bad, live in a state of consciousness. ... I believe that any of these spirits may according to the order of God, in the laws of their place of residence, hare intercourse with this world, and become visible to mortals." This doctrine is affirmed, from the reason that Samuel actually appeared to Saul; Moses and Elias talked with Jesus in the presence of Peter, James and John, and there are many other such instances recorded.

Dr. Richard Watson, of England, who was regarded as the most intellectual teacher the Methodist church ever had, referring to the case of Samuel, says: "The account not only shows that the Jews believed in the doctrine of apparitions, but that in fact such an appearance on this occasion did actually occur; which answers all the objections which were ever raised or can be raised, from the philosophy of the case, against the possibility of the appearance of departed spirits. I believe in this apparition of the departed Samuel, because the text positively calls the appearance Samuel."

In his *Theological Institutes*, a standard work embraced in the course of study for ministers, Dr. Watson says:

"This is the doctrine of revelation; and if the evidence of that revelation can be disproved, it may be rejected; if not, it must be admitted, whether any argumentative proof can be offered in its favor or not. That it is not unreasonable may be first established. That God who made us and who is a pure spirit, can not have immediate access to our thoughts, our affections, and our will, it would certainly be much more reasonable to deny than to admit; and if the great and universal Spirit possesses power, every physical objection at least, to the doctrine in question is removed, and finite, unbodied spirits may have the same kind of access to the mind of man, though not in so perfect and intimate degree. Before any natural impossibility can be urged against this intercourse of spirit with spirit, we must know what no philosopher, however deep his researches into the courses of the phenomena of the mind, has ever professed to know — the laws of perception, memory and association. We can suggest thoughts and reason, to each other, and thus mutually influence our wills and affections. We employ, for this purpose, the media of signs and words; but to contend that these are the only media through which thought can be conveyed to thought, or that spiritual beings cannot produce the same effects immediately, is to found an objection wholly upon our ignorance. All the reason which the case, considered in itself, affords, is certainly in favor of this opinion. We have access to each other's minds; we can suggest thoughts, raise affections, influence the wills of others; and analogy, therefore, favors the conclusion that, though by different and latent means, unbodied spirits have the same access to each other, and us."

Dr. Watson related a remarkable instance which serves to illustrate the views so forcibly expressed, which was published many years ago in the *Methodist Magazine*, and later in the *Baltimore Methodist Magazine*. A man and his wife by the name of James, both of whom died very suddenly, leaving a large estate, as was supposed without a will. There arose serious difficulty among the heirs about the property. James and his Wife came back (in the day time) and informed a lady where the will was, in a secret drawer, in a secretary. She informed the circuit preacher (a Mr. Mills), who went and found the will, and reconciled the parties.

Bishop Simpson said it seemed to him "as though he were walking on one side of the veil, and his departed son on the other. It is only a veil. These friends will be the first to greet you, their faces the first to flash upon you, as you pass into the invisible world. This takes away the fear of death. Departed spirits are not far above the earth, in some distant clime, but right upon the confines of this world."

Dr. Wilber Fisk says: "God has use or employment for all the creatures he has made — for every saint on earth, for every angel in heaven. Oh consoling doctrine! Angels are around us. The spirits of the departed good encamp about our pathway."

Indeed it is a happy thought, a belief that must keep the soul anchored by faith near to God, a realization that is worth all else in a dying hour. How many of us have stood by the bedside of a loved and sainted friend, when the shadows were falling, watching every change of expression as they marked the features with the light of joy, while the veil was being drawn, affording a glimpse of the beautiful beyond, and heard the sweet feeble voice utter exclamations of rapturous praise for a vision too sublime to be described? And have we not felt a sanctifying awe pervading the heart as if conscious that the atmosphere was full of ministering spirits? Ah! "I would not live always." These are serious thoughts and impression that the living delight to cling to, no matter what may be our opinions concerning the spiritual world.

How anxiously we inquire after the last faint expressions from the lips of dying saints, in the hope of more evidence confirming the faith in a blessed abode, where the soul shall live forever in ecstasy. Can any one doubt that Bishop McKendree recognized ministering spirits around his dying bed when he exclaimed:

> *"Bright angels are from glory come,*
> *They are around my bed,*
> *They are in my room,*
> *They wait to waft my spirit home."*

Can any one read the last days and the last hour, yea, the last minute of John Wesley's life, as recorded by Tyerman in his *Life and Times of Wesley*, vol. iii., beginning on page 651, without feeling enthused by rapturous joy expressed by the great man, or doubt that the same ministering spirits that he claimed attended him all through his most wonderful and eventful career, directing his course and warning him daily of some new persecution that was coming, were present, and beheld by him during the last moments as the veil was drawn, when he exclaimed, "I'll praise! I'll praise!" and then cried, "Farewell!" the last word he uttered. Then as Joseph Bradford was saying, "Lift up your heads, 0 ye gates; and be ye lifted up, ye everlasting doors, and this heir of glory shall come in!" Wesley gathered up his feet in the presence of his brethren, and without a groan and without a sigh was gone.

Indeed there must be something exceedingly comforting in this simple child-like fairly, and it does appear that no one need go astray as long as such faith is well poised in God, looking to Him always for spiritual guidance, rather than relying directly on apparitions, premonitions, and spiritual communications; a kind of self-righteousness, forgetting that God has any hand in the matter, and may permit bad spirits unrestrained, to deceive the believer.

Recurring once more to Saul, who had in his great zeal for God's cause, (or rather his own conceit) "put away those that had familiar spirits and the wizards out of the ]and," and would have slain the witch of Endor had he known of her, as she greatly feared, and cried with a loud voice when Samuel appeared, Saying, "Why hast thou deceived me? For thou art Saul," he was conscious of having disobeyed the voice of the Lord, in not executing His fierce wrath upon Amalek, and knew that God was angry and had withdrawn from him; and yet, in his sore distress, when the Philistines were upon him, he did not humble himself in the sight of God, imploring pardon and Divine aid. He simply "inquired of the Lord, and the Lord answered him not, neither by **dreams**, nor by **Urim**, nor by **prophets**." Saul no doubt thought it was God's business to direct him in saving Israel, and was sulky, and in his own strength, went in disguise to the witch he would have slain, "Wherefore then dost thou ask of me, seeing the Lord has departed from thee, and is become thine enemy," answered Samuel. Now mark two expressions in this chapter, Samuel xxiii. "What sawest thou?" inquired Saul. "And the woman said unto Saul, I saw **gods** ascending **out** of the **earth**." "An old man **cometh up**; he is covered with a mantle." It appears from this that the spirit of Samuel ascended **out** of the **earth** and came not from above. Again, Samuel said to Saul, "Moreover, the Lord will also deliver Israel with thee into the hands of the Philistines; and tomorrow shalt, thou and thy sons be with me." The question: Where was Samuel that Saul should be with him on "tomorrow" when he fell upon his own sword and was slain as prophesied? Samuel came up out of the earth and Saul was certainly not in favor with God, to warrant any belief in his ascension to heaven, if Samuel was.

Another reference, Daniel v., gives an account of the hand writing on the wall. Nebuchadnezzar, to whom God had given majesty and glory and honor, but when his heart was lifted up, and his mind hardened in pride, he was deposed and his glory taken from him, and he was driven from the sons of men and become as a beast fed with grass like oxen, till he knew that the most high God ruled in the kingdom of men. Belshazzar, his son and successor, knowing this, humbled not his heart, but made a great feast, drank wine and praised the gods of gold, and of silver, of brass, of iron, of wood, and of stone. This was not all; he had the consecrated vessels which his father Nebuchadnezzar had taken out of the Temple at Jerusalem and desecrated them in use in his drunken revelry. "In the same hour came forth fingers of a man's hand, and wrote over against the candlestick upon the plaster of the wall of the king's palace; and the king saw the part of the hand that wrote: "Then the king's' countenance was changed, and his thoughts troubled him, so that the joints of his loins were loosed, and his knees smote one against the other." None of the astrologers, the Chaldeans, soothsayers, or wise men of Babylon, could read or interpret the hand writing, and Daniel of the captivity who had an excellent spirit and knowledge, was brought before the king and read the hand writing, "Mene, mene, tekel, upharisin." The interpretation, "Thou are weighed in the balances and art found wanting." "In that night was Belshazzar the king of the Chaldeans slain." Again the question recurs, whose hand was this that wrote upon the wall? Many believe it was the hand of God, but the Bible says it was "fingers of man's hand." Daniel says "the part of the hand sent by Him," (God) and Daniel certainly knew, for he was the only one who could read and interpret, the writing. Then it was a man's hand and God sent it. Here again it is claimed that the doctrine of spiritual communication is sustained, and the laws of God being immutable, just what was done then can be done now; and therefore people cannot understand the many mysterious things that occur. But the moral: Belshazzar was not so much frightened by the hand writing on the wall, as he was by that inward conscience smiting on the wall of his heart, which awakened him to a sense of his guilt and condemnation, which caused his knees to tremble and smite each other. The handwriting was the warning of his doom, and that was what he wanted to know. There is not a wrong doer or sinner in this enlightened age, who has not felt this same smiting of the heart. Conscience is an all-powerful spirit that cannot be resisted though it may not be heeded until the handwriting appears off the wall.

We learn also from reading the Bible that there was another class of extremist, religious bigots, who believed that all spiritual communications were works of the devil, and they made laws to put mediums or witches to death. II. Kings xxiii, informs us of the great zeal of Josiah for the house of the Lord. In the eighteenth year of King Josiah the greatest Passover known in all the history of the

Jews was held to the Lord.

> "Moreover, the workers with familiar spirits and the wizards, and the images and the idols, and all the abominations that were spied in the land of Judah, and in Jerusalem, did Josiah put away, that he might perform the words of the law which were written in the book that Hilkiah the priest found in the house of the Lord. Notwithstanding, the Lord turned not from the fierceness of His great wrath, wherewith his anger was kindled against Judah."

This kind of zeal to please God in some other way than by the sacrifice of a contrite heart, and free communion with the spirit of the Most High, has characterized all ages, and down to the present time we find men who have come in possession of great fortunes by stealth and advantage, by which thousands have been impoverished, giving munificent gifts to charitable institutions in the hope of winning favor with God and gaining the praise of religious people, and whose funeral orations team with glowing accounts of their goodness in life. This was the kind of opposition that John Wesley had to contend with. He was reviled, hounded and vilified by the ablest ministers of the Church of England, books and pamphlets by the score were written, and newspapers engaged in ridiculing his religion. But the great man with a heart overflowing with the love of God and humanity, by a single mild utterance or the dash of his pen, turned all of their anathemas against them.

Witches were burnt at the stake in the name of the church, even in this country. The laws of Massachusetts made witchcraft an offense punishable by death, and the Puritans found no trouble in procuring the evidence to convict the accused. The first execution took place in Charlestown, Mass., in 1648; Margaret Jones was the victim, and John Winthrop, Governor of the State, presided at the condemning trial. Witchcraft was considered a crime against the laws of God, and the persecution continued, and many were put to death all along, but the great crusade occurred in February, 1692, at Salem, when the excitement reached its highest tension. Thirty women were convicted that year on the testimony of children, who claimed that they were tormented by the women; twenty of the number were executed.

Out of such intolerance came the necessity for religious liberty, a division of sentiment on Bible doctrines, and the formation of many sects or denominations into churches, and religious liberty has continued to broaden into a mighty spread of the gospel of Christ through the rivalry of denominations, or rather a spirit of emulation, each striving to do the most for the advancement of pure Christianity. But for these divisions and religious liberty, zealots would have been burning witches until yet. And if our churches could all be united into one, under one universal creed and laws of control, as some people desire, we would return to witch burning within fifty years. The world, and the churches as they are organized, are full of religious bigots, who have no patience with that class professing close communion with God through the medium of the spirit, because they themselves know nothing of such religion.

The Bible has much to say about evil spirits as well as good spirits, and all through Acts we find that Paul often came in contact with those having evil spirits and those who practiced witchcraft, sorcery, etc., but this the reader is familiar with, while there are many authenticated phenomena of later days that serve better for the present purpose. No one now doubts the authenticity of the Epworth ghost — "Jeffry." Rev. John Wesley published the whole story himself in the *Arminian Magazine* for October, November and December, 1784. The demonstrations commenced very much like the Bell Witch, by knocking and other noise just by Mr. Wesley's bed. For some time the Wesley family hooted at the idea of the supernatural, but investigation finally settled them in this conclusion beyond a doubt. It continued to gather force just as did the Bell Witch but never to the extent of talking or speaking. When spoken to, the answers were in groans and squeaks, but no intelligent utterance. It was seen several times and looked like a badger. The man servant chased it out of the dining room once, when it ran into the kitchen, and was like a white rabbit. Miss Susannah Wesley relates details which point to the presence of a disembodied Jacobite, the knocking being more violent at the words "our most Gracious Sovereign Lord," when applied to King George I, as generally used by Mr. Wesley in his prayers. This being noticed, when Mr. Wesley omitted prayer for the royal family no knocking occurred, which Mr. Wesley considered good evidence.

The *Review of Reviews*, New Year's extra number for 1892, which is devoted entirely to the scientific investigations of the Psychical Research Society, contains in its wide scope of investigations more than one hundred phenomena. The story of a haunted parsonage in the north of Eng land in which the phenomena occurred in 1891, the spirit was more demonstrative than the Epsworth ghost. The demonstrations consisted in

The rocking of Dr. William Smith's cradle, which occurred in 1840 in Lynchburg, Va., is a most remarkable and well authenticated phenomena. Dr. Smith was pastor of the Lynchburg church and many people Called to witness the strange action of the cradle, which commenced rocking of its own accord, and rocked one hour every day for thirty days. A committee was appointed to investigate the cause, and the cradle was taken to pieces and examined, every part and put together again, and transferred to different rooms, and it rocked all the same without any hand touching it. Rev. Dr. Penn undertook to hold it still, and it wrenched itself from his hands, the timber cracking as if it would break in his firm grasp.

Thousands of such phenomena, premonitions, etc., well authenticated, might be cited, but there is nothing on record, or in all history of phenomena outside of the Bible, that equals the deeply mysterious demonstrations of the Bell Witch — seemingly a thing of life, like that of a human being, endowed with mind, speech, and superior knowledge, knowing all things, all men, and their inmost thoughts and secret deeds, a thing of physical power and force superior to that of the stoutest man — action as swift as the lightning, and yet invisible and incomprehensible.

Spiritualists undertake to account for such mysteries, but theirs is a very dangerous doctrine for the ordinary mind to tamper with. One is liable to lose sight of God and repose faith in the medium, who is but a human being, and if possessed with power to communicate with spirits, may communicate with evil as well as good spirits. Moreover, it is destructive to an unbalanced mind. All people possess more or less animal electricity or magnetism, which is more largely developed in one than in another, and always more in the medium, whose will power overbalances the other. This force, however, is developed in the practice of methods of communication, and involves the whole mind and will power, convulsing the mind into an abnormal state, subjected to the electric force. Persons who will sit for one hour daily, with their hands on a table, giving all attention to spiritual manifestations, will, on rising, feel a tingling nervous sensation in their arms, and all through the system, which should not be cultivated. It is better that such investigations be left to the Society of Psychological Research, scientific men of strong minds who have nothing else to do but to demonstrate, if they can, the theory that all such mysteries are hidden in the yet mysterious electrical force that permeates the atmosphere, the earth and all animal nature, and which is being brought into use, developing some new power or force every day, and prove that we are nearing a spiritual kingdom where the disembodied are to be seen and conversed with.

Man is constituted a worshipping being, consequently all men are superstitious, notwithstanding that, nine out of ten will deny most emphatically holding to any kind of superstition. Yet when put to the test not one of common intelligence can be found who has not seen something, or heard something, dreamed something, or experienced premonitions, that left an impress of the mysterious. For instance, a gentleman familiar with the history of the Bell Witch, discussing it with the writer, declared that those old people were superstitious, and he did not believe a word of it; that there was not a particle of superstition in his composition; "yet," said he, "there was something unaccountable at Bell's, no doubt about that." Did he believe it? Why certainly. Another instance: A very able, pious minister, discussing the same subject in connection with the Wesley haunt, said he did not believe a word of such things; it was all spiritualism, misleading and dangerous, and Wesley, great man as he was, was liable to such mistakes in an abnormal state of mind. Then he related an incident in the early settlement of the country, when our fathers came among the red men. Said he: "My grandfather belonged to the Nashville settlement; he dreamed that the Indians had attacked the little fort in Sumner county, while the inmates were asleep, and killed everyone. He was awakened by the force of the presentment, yet thought nothing of it, and fell asleep again, and dreamed the same thing, the premonition coming the second time with still more force. He was greatly agitated, and mounted his best horse, as quick as he could, running the horse every jump of the way to the little fort. Arriving he found everybody sound asleep, and aroused the people in great haste, shouting in the camp that Indians were marching on the fort, and the settlers had barely made ready when the enemy attacked. The citizens won the victory, routing the Indians without loss. But for the dream and grandfather's prompt action, the last one in the fort would have been slain." Is this excellent gentleman, believing his grandfather's story, as he certainly does, free from superstition? Summing up the whole matter, it is useless and silly to condemn that which we know nothing about and cannot understand or explain. It is an assumption of wisdom that discredits our intelligence, and the best way to treat ghosts is to let them alone, never go spook hunting, but if a spirit comes to us, receive it just as a spirit deserves to be treated, and observe the warning on the wall, whether it be written by the hand of a spectre, or indicted by the finger of conscience.

# Chapter 8

## *Our Family Trouble: The Story of the Bell Witch as Detailed by Richard Williams Bell*

The reader is already familiar with the motives that inspired Richard Williams Bell to write this sketch of "Our Family Trouble," a phenomenal mystery that continued to be a living sensation long after John Bell's death, the mention of which in any Robertson County family, even to this good day, leads to a recital of events as they have been handed down through tradition.

After a brief biography of his parents and the family, which is more fully recorded elsewhere, Mr. Bell goes on writing:

After settling on Red River in Robertson County, Tenn., my father prospered beyond his own expectations. He was a good manager, and hard worker himself, making a regular hand on the farm. He indulged no idleness around him, and brought up his children to work, endeavoring to make their employment pleasurable. Mother was equally frugal and careful in her domestic affairs, and was greatly devoted to the proper moral training of children, keeping a restless watch over everyone, making sacrifices for their pleasure and well being, and both were steadfast in their religious faith, being members of the Baptist church, and set Christian examples before their children. Father was always forehanded, paid as he went, was never in his life served with a warrant or any legal process, and never had occasion to fear the sheriff or any officer of the law, and was equally faithful in bearing his share of whatever burden was necessary to advance morality and good society. In the meanwhile he gave all of his children the best education the schools of the country could afford, Zadok being educated for a lawyer, while the other boys chose to follow agriculture. Jesse and Esther had both married, settled, and everything seemed to be going smoothly, when our trouble commenced. I was a boy when the incidents, which I am about to record, known as the Bell Witch took place. In fact, strange appearances and uncommon sounds had been seen and heard by different members of the family at times, some year or two before I knew anything about it, because they indicated nothing of a serious character, gave no one any concern, and would have passed unnoticed but for after developments. Even the knocking on the door, and the outer walls of the house, had been going on for some time before I knew of it, generally being asleep, and father, believing that it was some mischievous person trying to frighten the family, never discussed the matter in the presence of the younger children, hoping to catch the prankster. Then, after the demonstrations became known to all of us, father enjoined secrecy upon every member of the family, and it was kept a profound secret until it became intolerable. Therefore no notes were made of these demonstrations or the exact dates. The importance of a diary at that time did not occur to any one, for we were all subjected to the most intense and painful excitement from day to day, and week to week, to the end, not knowing from whence came the disturber, the object of the visitation, what would follow next, how long it would continue, nor the probable result. Therefore I write from memory, such things as came under my own observations, impressing my mind, and incidents known by other members of the family and near neighbors to have taken place, and are absolutely true. However, I do not pretend to record the half that did take place, for that would be impossible without daily notes, but will note a sufficient number of incidents to give the reader a general idea of the phenomena and the afflictions endured by our family.

As before stated, the knocking at the door, and scratching noise on the outer wall, which continued so long, never disturbed me, nor was I the least frightened until the demonstrations within became unendurable. This I think was in May, 1818. Father and mother occupied a room on the first floor, Elizabeth had the room above, and the boys occupied another room on the second floor; John and Drewry had a bed together, and Joel and myself slept in another bed. As I remember it was on Sunday night, just after the family had retired, a noise commenced in our room like a rat gnawing vigorously on the bed post. John and Drew got up to kill the rat. But the moment they were out of bed the noise ceased. They examined the bedstead, but discovered no marks made by a rat. As soon as they returned to bed the noise commenced again, and thus it continued until a late hour or some time after midnight, and we were all up a half dozen times or more searching the room all over, every nook and corner, for the rat, turning over everything, and could find nothing, not even a crevice by which a rat could possibly enter. This kind of noise continued from night to night, and week after week, and all of our investigations were in vain. The room was overhauled several times, everything moved and carefully examined, with the same result. Finally when we would search for the rat in our room, the same noise would appear in sister Elizabeth's chamber, disturbing her, and arousing all the family. And so it continued going from room to room, stopping when we were all up, and commencing again as soon as we returned: to bed, and was so exceedingly annoying that no one could sleep. The noise was, after a while, accompanied by a scratching sound, like a dog clawing on the floor, and increased in force until it became evidently too strong for a rat. Then every room in the house was torn up, the furniture, beds and clothing carefully examined, and still nothing irregular could be found, nor was there a hole or crevice by which a rat could enter, and nothing was accomplished beyond the increase of our confusion and evil forebodings. The demonstrations continued to increase, and finally the bed covering commenced slipping off at the foot of the beds as if gradually drawn by someone, and occasionally a noise like the smacking of lips, then a gulping sound, like someone choking or strangling, while the vicious gnawing at the bed post continued, and there was no such thing as sleep to be thought of until the noise ceased, which was generally between one and three o'clock in the morning. Some new performance was added nearly every night, and it troubled Elizabeth more than anyone else. Occasionally the sound was like heavy stones falling on the floor, then like trace chains dragging, and chairs falling over. I call to mind my first lively experience, something a boy is not likely to forget. We bad become somewhat used to the mysterious noise, and tried to dismiss it from mind, taking every opportunity for a nap. The family had all retired early, and I had just fallen into a sweet doze, when I felt my hair beginning to twist, and then a sudden jerk, which raised me. It felt like the top of my head had been taken off. Immediately Joel yelled out in great fright, and next Elizabeth was screaming in her room, and ever after that something was continually pulling at her hair after she retired to bed. This transaction frightened us so badly that father and mother remained up nearly all night.

After this, the main feature in the phenomenon was that of pulling the cover off the beds as fast as we could replace it, also continuing other demonstrations. Failing in all efforts to discover the source of the annoyance, and becoming convinced that it was something out of the natural course of events, continually on the increase in force, father finally determined to solicit the cooperation of Mr. James Johnson, who was his nearest neighbor and most intimate friend, in trying to detect the mystery, which had been kept a secret within the family up to this time. So Mr. Johnson and wife, at father's request, came over to spend a night in the investigation. At the usual hour for retiring, Mr. Johnson, who was a very devout Christian, led in family worship, as was his custom, reading a chapter in the Bible, singing and praying. He prayed fervently, and very earnestly for our deliverance from the frightful disturbance, or that its origin, cause and purpose might be revealed. Soon after we had all retired, the disturbance commenced as usual; gnawing, scratching, knocking on the wall, overturning chairs, pulling the cover off of beds, etc., every act being exhibited as if on purpose to show Mr. Johnson what could he done, appearing in his room, as in other rooms, and so soon as a light would appear, the noise would cease, and the trouble begin in another room.

Mr. Johnson listened attentively to all of the sounds and capers, and that which appeared like someone sucking air through the teeth, and smacking of lips, indicated to him that some intelligent agency gave force to the movements, and he determined to try speaking to it, which he did, inquiring, "In the name of the Lord, what or who are you? What do you want and why are you here?" This appeared to silence the noise for considerable time, but it finally returned with increased vigor, pulling the cover from the beds in spite of all resistance, repeating other demonstrations, going from one room to another, becoming fearful. The persecutions of Elizabeth were increased to an extent that excited serious apprehensions. Her cheeks were frequently crimsoned as by a hard blow from an open hand, and her hair pulled until she would scream with pain.

Mr. Johnson said the phenomenon was beyond his comprehension; it was evidently preternatural or supernatural, of an intelligent character. He arrived at this conclusion from the fact that it ceased action when spoken to, and certainly understood language. He advised father to invite other friends into the investigation, and to try all means for detecting the mystery, to which he consented, and from this time on, it became public.

All of our neighbors were invited and committees formed, experiments tried, and a close watch kept, in and out, every night, but all of their wits were stifled, the demon and kind to her in this trying ordeal. It was suggested that sister should spend the nights with some one of the neighbors to get rid of the trouble, and all were very kind to invite her. In fact our neighbors were all touched with generous sympathy and were unremitting in their efforts to alleviate our distress, for it had become a calamity, and they came every night to sit and watch with us. The suggestion of sending Elizabeth from home was acted upon. She went to different places, James Johnson's, John Johnson's, Jesse Bell's, and Bennett Porter's, but it made no difference, the trouble followed her with the same severity, disturbing the family where she went as it did at home, nor were we in anywise relieved. This gave rise to a suspicion in the minds of some persons that the mystery was some device or stratagem originated by sister, from the fact that it appeared wherever she went, and this clue was followed to a logical demonstration of the phenomena was gradually developed, proving to be an intelligent character. When asked a question in a way, that it could be answered by numbers, for instance, "How many persons present? How many horses in the barn? How many miles to a certain place?" The answers would come in raps, like a man knocking on the wall, the bureau or the bedpost with his fist, or by so many scratches on the wall like the noise of a nail or claws, and the answers were invariably correct. During the time, it was not uncommon to see lights like a candle or lamp flitting across the yard and through the field, and frequently when father, the boys and hands were coming in late from work, chunks of wood and stones would fall along the way as if tossed by someone, but we could never discover from whence, or what direction they came. In addition to the demonstrations already described, it took to slapping people on the face, especially those who resisted the action of pulling the cover from the bed, and those who came as detectives to expose the trick. The blows were heard distinctly, like the open palm of a heavy hand, while the sting was keenly felt, and it did not neglect to pull my hair, and make Joel squall as often.

## The Witch Commenced Whispering

The phenomena continued to develop force, and visitors persisted in urging the witch to talk, and tell what was wanted, and finally it commenced whistling when spoken to, in a low broken sound, as if trying to speak in a whistling voice, and in this way it progressed, developing until the whistling sound was changed to a weak faltering whisper uttering indistinct words. The voice, however, gradually gained strength in articulating, and soon the utterances became distinct in a low whisper, so as to be understood in the absence of any other noise. I do not remember the first intelligent utterance, which, however, was of no significance, but the voice soon developed sufficient strength to be distinctly heard by everyone in the room.

## A Disturbed Spirit

This new development added to the sensation already created. The news spread, and people came in larger numbers, and the great anxiety concerning the mystery prompted many questions in the effort to induce the witch to disclose its own identity and purpose. Finally, in answer to the question, "Who are you and what do you want?" the reply came, "I am a spirit; I was once very happy but have been disturbed." This was uttered in a very feeble voice, but sufficiently distinct to be understood by all present, and this was all the information that could be elicited for the time.

## The Seer's Prophecy

The next utterance of any note that I remember, occurred on a Sunday night, when the voice appeared stronger, and the witch talking more freely, in fact speaking voluntarily, and appeared to be exercised over a matter that was being discussed by the family. Brother John Bell had for some time contemplated a trip to North Carolina to look after father's share of an estate that was being wound up, and was to start next morning (Monday) on horseback, and this was the matter that interested the family and was being discussed, the long tiresome journey, his probable long absence, the situation of affairs, concerning which father was giving him instructions. Several neighbors were present, taking an interest, volunteering some good natured advice to John, when the witch put in, remonstrating against the trip, dissuading John from going, predicting bad luck, telling him that he would have a hard trip for nothing, that the estate had not been wound up and could not be for some time, and be would get no money, but return empty handed. As a further argument to dissuade John, the witch told him that an elegant young lady from Virginia was then on her way to visit friends in Robertson county, who would please him, and he could win her if he would stay; that she was wealthy, possessing forty Negroes and considerable money. John laughed at the revelation as supremely ridiculous, and left on the following morning as contemplated, and was absent six months or more, returning empty handed as predicted. Very soon after his departure, the young lady in question arrived, and left before his return, and John never met her.

## A Spirit Hunting a Lost Tooth

The witch continued, to develop the power of articulation, talking freely, and those who engaged in conversation with the invisible persevered in plying questions t6draw out an explanation of the mystery, and again the question was pressed, inquiring, "Who are you and what do you want?" and the witch replied, stating the second time, "I am a spirit who was once very happy, but have been disturbed and made unhappy." Then followed the question, "How were you disturbed, and what makes you unhappy?" The reply to this question was, "I am the spirit of a person who was buried in the woods near by, and the grave has been disturbed, my bones disinterred and scattered, and one of my teeth was lost under this house, and I am here looking for that tooth."

This statement revived the memory of a circumstance that occurred some three or four years previously, and had been entirely forgotten. The farm hands while engaged in clearing a plot of land, discovered a small mound of graves, which father supposed to be an Indian burying ground, and worked around it without obliterating the marks. Several days later Corban Hall, a young man of the neighborhood, came to our place, and was told by Drew the circumstance of finding the Indian graves. Hall thought the graves probably contained some relics which Indians commonly buried with their dead, and proposed to open one and see, to which Drew agreed, and they proceeded to disinter the bones. Finding nothing else, Hall brought the jawbone to the house, and while sitting in the passage he threw it against the opposite wall, and the jarring knocked out a loose tooth, which dropped through a crack in the floor.

Father passed through the hall in the meanwhile, and reprimanded the boys severely for their action, and made one of the Negro men take the jawbone back, replacing all the disinterred bones, and filling in the grave. This was evidently the circumstance referred to by the "spirit," so long forgotten, and to be reminded of the fact so mysteriously was very perplexing, and troubled father no little. He examined the floor just where the bone dropped when it struck the wall, as the boys had left it, and there was the crack referred to, and he was pestered, and decided to take up a portion of the floor and see if the tooth could be found. The dirt underneath was raked up, sifted and thoroughly exam ined, but the tooth was not found. The witch then laughed at father, declaring that it was all a joke to fool "Old Jack."

## The Buried Treasure

The excitement in the country increased as the phenomena developed, The fame of the witch had become widely spread, and people came from all quarters to hear the strange and unaccountable voice.

Some were detectives, confident of exposing the mystery. Various opinions were formed and expressed; some credited its own story, and believed it an Indian spirit; some thought it was an evil spirit, others declared it was witchcraft, and a few unkindly charged that it was magic art and trickery gotten up by the Bell family to draw crowds and make money. These same people had stayed as long as they wished, enjoyed father's hospitality, and paid not a cent for it, nor did it ever cost any one a half shilling. The house was open to everyone that came; father and mother gave them the best they had, their horses were fed, and no one allowed to go away hungry; many offered pay and urged father to receive it, insisting that he could not keep up entertaining so many without pay, but he persistently declined remuneration, and not one of the family ever received a cent for entertaining. Father regarded the phenomena as an affliction, a calamity, and such accusations were very galling, but were endured. Inquisitive people continued to exercise all of their wits in plying the witch with questions concerning, its personality or character, but elicited no further information until the question was put by James Gunn, then came the reply: "I am the spirit of an early emigrant, who brought a large sum of money and buried my treasure for safe keeping until needed. In the meanwhile I died without divulging the secret, and I have returned in the spirit for the purpose of making known the hiding place, and I want Betsy Bell to have the money." The spirit was then urged to tell where the money was concealed. This was refused and the secret withheld until certain pledges were made that the conditions would be complied with. The conditions were that Drew Bell and Bennett Porter would agree to exhume the money and give every dollar to Betsy, and that "Old Sugar Mouth" (Mr. James Johnson) would go with them and see that the injunction was fairly discharged, and that he should count the money and take charge of it for Betsy. The story was questioned and laughed at, and then discussed. The witch had made some remarkable revelations, and it was thought possible there might be something in it, and the proposition was acceded to. Drew and Bennett agreed to do the work, and Mr. Johnson consented to become the guardian and see that the right thing was done. The spirit then went on. to state that the money was under a large flat rock at the mouth of the spring on the southwest corner of the farm, on Red River, describing the surroundings so minutely that there could be no mistake. Everyone was acquainted with the spring, having frequented the place, but no one could have described it so minutely, and this all tended to strengthen faith in the revelation. The spirit insisted that the committee selected should start very early the next morning at the dawn of day, lest the secret should get out, and some fiend should beat them to the place and get the money. This was also agreed to, and by the break of day next morning all hands met and proceeded to the spring. They found everything as described, the huge stone intact, and were sure they were on time. They observed that it was an excellent place for hiding money where no human being would ever dream of looking for a treasure, or care to move the great stone for any purpose, and yet susceptible of such a minute description that no one could be mistaken in the revelation. They carried along an axe and mattock, and were pretty soon at work, devising ways and means for moving the big rock, which was so firmly imbedded in the ground. It was no light job, but they cut poles, made levers and fixed prizes, after first removing much dirt from around the stone, so as to get under it. Then Drew and Porter prized and tugged, Mr. Johnson occasionally lending a helping hand, and after a half day's very hard work, the stone was raised and moved from its bedding, but no money appeared. Then followed a consultation and discussion of the situation. They reasoned that the glittering treasure was possibly sunk in the earth, and the stone imbedded over it to elude suspicion, and they decided to dig for it, and went to work in earnest, Porter digging, and Drew scratching the loosened dirt out with his hands, and so on they progressed until they had opened a hole about six feet square and nearly as many feet deep, and still no money was found. Exhausted and very hungry, they gave up the job, returning to the house late in the afternoon much disgusted and chagrined. That night the "spirit" appeared in great glee laughing and tantalizing the men for being so easily duped, describing everything that occurred at the spring in the most ludicrous way, telling how they tugged at the big stone, and repeating what was said by each one. Bennett Porter staved the mattock in up to the eye every pop, and oh how it made him sweat. It told how "Old Sugar Mouth" looked on prayerfully, encouraging the boys. The dirt taken out was mixed with small stones, gravel, sand, etc., leaves and sticks, all of which indicated that the earth had been removed and put back. Drew, the witch said, could handle a sight of dirt, his hands were made for that purpose, and were better than a shovel; no gold could slip through his fingers. The witch's description of the affair kept the house in an uproar of laughter, and it was repeated with equal zest to all new comers for a month.

## Priest Craft and Scriptural Knowledge

There were but very few churches in the country at this period of the century, nevertheless, ours was a very religious community. Most of those coming from the older States brought their religion with them, and inculcated the principle in their families. The influence of Revs. James and Thomas Gunn, Rev. Sugg Fort, Mr. James Johnson, and other good men, swayed mightily. Every man erected an altar in his own home, and it was common for neighbors to meet during the week at one or another's house for prayer and exhortation, and Bible study. In the absence of the preachers, Mr. James Johnson was the principal leader in these exercises, and the meetings were held alternately at his house and father's, and occasionally at one or the other of the Gunn's. There was no spirit of denominational jealousy existing, and all Christians mingled in these meetings like brethren of the same faith. The witch, as it accumulated force, dissembled this spirit, giving wonderful exhibitions of a thorough knowledge of the Bible and Christian faith. The voice was not confined to darkness, as were the physical demonstrations. The talking was heard in lighted rooms, as in the dark; and finally in the day at any hour. The first exhibition of a religious nature was the assimilation of Mr. James Johnson's character and worship, repeating the song and prayer, uttering precisely the same petition made by the old gentleman the night himself and wife came for the purpose of investigation, and the impersonation of Mr. Johnson was so perfect that it appeared like himself present. It was not uncommon after this for the witch to introduce worship, by lining a hymn, as was the custom, singing it through, and then repeat Mr. Johnson's prayer, or the petitions of some one of the ministers. It could sing any song in the hymn books of that time, and quote any passage of Scripture in the Bible from Genesis to Revelations. The propensity for religious discussion was strongly manifested, and in quoting Scripture the text was invariably correctly cited, and if any one misquoted a verse, they would be promptly corrected. It could quote Scripture as fast as it could talk, one text after another, citing the book, chapter, and number of the verse. It was a common test to open the Bible at any chapter, and call on the spirit to repeat a certain verse, and this was done accurately, as fast as the leaves were turned from one chapter of the book to another. It delighted in taking issue on religious subjects, with those well versed in Scripture, and was sure to get the best of the argument, being always quick with a passage to sustain its point. This manifest knowledge of Scripture on the part of the witch was unmistakable, and was the most mystifying of all the developments, and strangers who came from a long distance were eager to engage the seer in religious discussions, and were is often confounded; and they were no less astounded when the witch would remind them of events and circumstances in their history in a way that was marvelous. Just here one circumstance I call to mind. The discussion had turned on the command against covetousness and theft. A man, whose name I will call John, put in remarking that he did not believe there was any sin in stealing something to eat when one was reduced to hunger, and could not obtain food for his labor. Instantly the witch perniciously inquired of John "if he ate that sheepskin." This settled John. He was dumb as an oyster, and as soon as the subject was changed he left the company, and was conspicuously absent after that. The result was the revival of an old scandal, so long past that it had been forgotten, in which John was accused of stealing a sheepskin. This warlock was indeed a great tattler, and made mischief in the community. Some people very much feared the garrulity of its loquacious meddling and were extremely cautious, and it was this class who the invisible delighted in torturing most. Nothing of moment occurred in the country or in any family, which was not reported by the witch at night. The development of this characteristic led the people to inquire after the news and converse with the witch as they would with a person, very often inquiring what was then transpiring at a certain place or house in the neighborhood. Sometimes the answer would be, "I don't know, wait a minute and I will go and see," and in less than five minutes it would report, and the report was generally verified. This feature of the phenomena was discovered in this way: Brother Jesse Bell lived within one mile of the homestead. He had been absent several days on a trip, and was expected home on a certain evening. After supper mother entered the room, inquiring if any of us knew whether Jesse had returned or not. No one had heard, or could inform her. The witch manifested much regard for mother on all occasions, and never afflicted her in any way. On this occasion it spoke promptly, saying: "Wait a minute Luce, I will go and see for you." Scarcely a minute had elapsed when the voice reported that Jesse was at home, describing his position, sitting at table reading by the light of a candle. The next morning Jesse came to see us, and when told the circumstance, he said it was true, and just at that time there was a distinct rap on his door, and before he could move the door opened and closed immediately. His wife, he said, noticed it also, and asked me what caused it, and I replied that I reckoned it was the witch. Every

Sabbath service that occurred within the bounds was reported at night, the text, hymn, etc., and the preacher also criticized, and everything of peculiar note was described. The company was treated one night to a repetition of one of Rev. James Gunn's best sermons, preached in the vicinity, the witch personating Mr. Gunn, lining the hymn, quoting his text and prayer, and preaching so much like Mr. Gunn, that it appeared the minister himself was present.

A number of persons were present who attended the meeting that day, and recognized the declamation as the same sermon. Shortly after this, Rev. James Gunn preached on Sunday at Bethel Methodist Church, six miles southeast, and Rev. Sugg Fort filled his appointment at Drake's Pond Baptist Church, seven miles north-west, thirteen miles apart, both preaching at the same hour, eleven o'clock. It so happened that both ministers came to visit our family that evening, finding quite a crowd of people gathered in, as was the case every day during the excitement. Directly after supper the witch commenced talking as usual, directing the conversation to Brother Gunn, discussing some points in his sermon that day. Mr. Gunn asked the witch how it knew what he had preached about? The answer was, "I was present and heard you." This statement being questioned, the "vociferator" began, quoted the text and repeated the sermon verbatim, and the closing prayer, all of which the preacher said was correct. Someone suggested that Brother Fort had the advantage of the witch this time, that having attended Brother Gunn's service, it could tell nothing about Brother Fort's discourse at Drake's Pond. "Yes I can," was the prompt reply. How do you know? was the inquiry. "I was there and heard him." Then assimilating Rev. Fort's style, it proceeded to quote his text and repeated his sermon, greatly delighting the company. There was no one present who had heard either sermon, but both ministers admitted that their sermons had been accurately reproduced, and no one could doubt the fact, or were more greatly surprised than themselves.

## The Afflictions of Betsy and Father

The reader will understand that no feature of the exhibitions al-ready introduced was ever abandoned, but continued developing virulence, or beneficence and felicity. The practice of pulling the cover off the beds was a favorite pastime, and frequently the sheets would be pulled from under the sleepers, or the pillows jerked from under their heads, and other new performances added to the exhibitions. The most serious consequence, however, was the afflictions of Elizabeth and father. Notwithstanding the invisible agency feigned a tender regard at times for Betsy, as it affectionately called her, it did not cease tormenting in many ways, increasing her punishment. The feint pretext for this was a manifest opposition to the attention paid her by a certain young gentleman, who was much esteemed by the family, often interposing impertinent objections, urging that these mutual relations be severed. At least there was no other cause manifested, or this would not be mentioned. Sister was now subjected to fainting spells, followed by prostration, characterized by shortness of breath and smothering sensations, panting as it were for life, and becoming entirely exhausted and lifeless, losing her breath for nearly a minute between gasps, and was rendered unconscious. She would revive and then relapse, and it appeared that her suffering was prolonged by the greater exertions used for her restoration. These spells lasted from thirty to forty minutes, and passed off suddenly, leaving her perfectly restored after a few minutes in which she recovered from the exhaustion. There is no positive evidence that these spells were produced by the witch. However, that was the conclusion, from the fact that there was no other apparent cause. She was a very stout girl, and with this exception, the personification of robust health, and was never subject to hysteria or anything of the kind. Moreover, the spells came on at regular hours in the evening, just at the time the witch usually appeared, and immediately after the spells passed off the mysterious voice commenced talking, but never uttered a word during the time of her prostration. In the meanwhile father was strangely afflicted, which should have been mentioned in the outset, but he had never regarded his trouble as of any consequence until after sister recovered from the attacks just described. In fact his ailment commenced with the incipiency of the witch demonstration, or before he recognized the phenomenal disturbance. He complained of a curious sensational feeling in his mouth, a stiffness of the tongue, and something like a stick crosswise, punching each side of his jaws. This sensation did not last long, did not recur very often, or cause pain, and therefore gave him but little concern. But as the phenomena developed, this affliction increased, his tongue swelling from the sides and pressing against his jaws, so that he could neither talk nor eat for ten or fifteen hours. In the meanwhile the witch manifested a pernicious dislike for father, using the most vile and malignant epithets toward him, declaring that it would torment "Old Jack Bell" to the end of his life. As father's trouble increased, Elizabeth was gradually relieved from her severe spells, and soon recovered entirely from the affliction, and never had another symptom of the kind. But father was seized with another malady that caused him much trouble and suffering. This was contortions of the face, a twitching and dancing of his flesh, which laid him up for the time. These spells gradually increased, and undoubtedly carried him to his grave, of which I will have more to say further on.

## The Witch Named "Kate"

People continued to ply our loquacious visitor with shrewd eager questions, trying to elicit some information concerning the mystery, which were with equal dexterity evaded, or a misleading answer given. First, it was a disturbed spirit hunting a lost tooth; next, a spirit that had returned to reveal the hiding place of a buried treasure. Then it told Calvin Johnson that it was the spirit of a child buried in North Caro lina, and told John Johnson that it was his step mother's witch. At last Rev. James Gunn manifested a very inquisitive desire to penetrate the greatest of all secrets, and put the question very earnestly. The witch replied, saying that Brother Gunn had put the question in a way that it could no longer be evaded, and it would not do to tell the preacher a flat lie, and if the plain truth must be known, it was nobody else and nothing but "Old Kate Batts' witch," determined to torment "Old Jack Bell" out of his life. This was a startling announcement and most unfortunate under the circumstances, because too many were willing to believe it, and it created a profound sensation. Mrs. Kate Batts was the wife of Frederick Batts, who was terribly afflicted, and she had become the head of the family, taking charge of her husband's affairs. She was very eccentric and sensitive. Some people were disposed to shun her, which was still more irritating to her sensitive nature. No harm could be said of Mrs. Batts. She was kind hearted, and a good neighbor toward those she liked. Mr. Gunn, of course, did not believe the witch's statement, but many did, or professed to, and the matter made Mrs. Batts very mad, causing a lively sensation in the community. Ever after this the goblin was called "Kate," and answered readily when addressed by that name, and for convenience sake I shall hereafter call the witch Kate, though not out of any disregard for the memory of Mrs. Batts, for after all she was a clever lady, and did not deserve the cruel appellation of "witch."

# The Witch Family — Blackdog, Mathematics, Cypocryphy, and Jerusalem

The next development was the introduction of four characters, assuming the above names, purporting to be a witch family, each one acting a part making night hideous in their high carnivals, using the most offensive language and uttering vile threats. Up to this time the strange visitor had spoken in the same soft delicate voice, except when personating some individual. Now there were four distinct voices. Blackdog assumed to be the head of the family, and spoke in a harsh feminine tone. The voices of Mathematics and Cypocryphy were different, but both of a more delicate feminine tone. Jerusalem spoke like a boy. These exhibitions were opened like a drunken carousal, and became perfect pandemoniums, frightful to the extreme, from which there was no escape. Father would most gladly have abandoned home and everything and fled with his family to some far away scene to have escaped this intolerable persecution, but there was no hope, no escape. The awful thing had sworn vengeance, and for what cause it never named, nor could any one ever surmise. Nevertheless, when the question of moving was discussed, it declared it would follow "Old Jack" to the remotest part of the earth, and father believed it. The family was frightened into consternation, apprehending that a terrible crisis was rapidly approaching. Many of our neighbors were frightened away, fearing they would become involved in a tragic termination. Others, however, drew nearer, and never forsook us in this most trying ordeal. James Johnson and his two sons, John and Calvin, the Gunn families, the Fort's, Gooch, William Porter, Frank Miles, Jerry Batts, Major Bartlett, Squire Byrns and Major Picketing were faithful and unremitting in their sympathy, and attentions, and consolations, making many sacrifices for our comfort, and not a night passed that four or more were not present to engage the witch in conversation, and relieve father of the necessary attention to strangers, giving him much rest. These demoniac councils were introduced by singing songs of every character, followed by quarreling with each other, employing obscene language and blasphemous oaths, making a noise like a lot of drunken men fighting. At this stage of the proceedings Blackdog would appear as peacemaker, denouncing the others with vehemence and scurrility, uttering bitter curses and threats of murder unless the belligerents should desist and behave themselves, and sometimes would apparently thrash Jerusalem unmercifully for disobeying orders. These carousals were ended only by the command of Blackdog, professedly sending the family away on different errands of deviltry, one or two remaining to keep up the usual disturbance in different rooms at the same time. On one occasion all four appeared almost beastly drunk, talking in a maudlin sentimental strain, fuming the house with the scent of whiskey. Blackdog said they got the whiskey at John Gardner's still house, which was some four miles distant. At other times the unity appeared more civil, and would treat our company to some delightful singing, a regular concert of rich feminine voices, modulated to the sweetest cadence and intonation, singing any hymn called for with solemnity and wonderful effect. The carousals did not continue long, much to the gratification of the family and friends, and our serious apprehensions were relieved. These concerts were agreeable closing exercises of this series of meetings, and after they were suspended the four demons or unity never, apparently, met again. It was plain old Kate from that time on who assumed all characters, good or bad, sometimes very pious and then extremely wicked.

## The Witch and the Negroes

Kate manifested a strong aversion for the Negro, often remarking, "I despise to smell a nigger, the scent makes me sick," and this no doubt accounts for the fact that the Negroes were never molested in their cabins after night, but away from their quarters they encountered a sight of trouble. Kate's repugnance was mutual; the Negroes disliked the witch, and were careful to evade all contacts possible by staying in after night, augmenting that natural odor peculiar to the race that was now worth something. They were afraid of the witch, and it was difficult to get one out for an emergency.

This fear was increased by the miraculous stories told by Dean, who was a kind of autocrat among the darkles, and by the way, was a good Negro, father's main reliance for heavy work, and noted for his skill with the axe and maul and wedge. He was worth two ordinary men in a forest clearing. Dean could see the witch any time when alone, or on his way to visit his wife, who belonged to Alex Gunn. It appeared to him, he said, in the form of a black dog, and sometimes had two heads, and at other times no head. The Negroes would stand around him with eyes and mouth wide open to hear his description of the witch, his encounters and hair breadth escapes. He always carried his axe and a witch ball made by his wife, according to Uncle Zeke's directions, to keep the witch from harming him. He came up one morning, however, rather worsted, with his head badly bruised and bloody, and always declared that the witch inflicted the wound with a stick. Dean's stories are not to be quoted as altogether reliable; he was allowed a wide range for his vivid imagination.

Harry, the houseboy, however, had cause for believing every word Dean told. It was Harry's business to make the morning fires before daylight. He became negligent in this duty, and father scolded and threatened him several times. Finally Kate took the matter in hand, speaking to father, "Never mind, old Jack, don't fret. I will attend to the rascal the next time he is belated." This passed off like much of such gab, but a few mornings after, Harry was later than ever and father commenced scolding harshly, when the witch spoke again, "Hold on old Jack, didn't I tell you not to pester; I will attend to this nigger." Harry had just laid the kindling wood down, and was on his knees blowing the coals to a blaze; when some unseen force apparently seized him by the neck and flailed him unmercifully. Harry yelled and begged piteously, and when let up the witch spoke, promising to repeat the operation if he was ever derelict again. Father said he heard the blows as they fell with force, sounding like a paddle or strip of wood, but could see nothing but the boy on his knees yelling for life. Harry was never late after that.

A rather funny trick was played on Phillis, a twelve year old girl who waited in the house and assisted her mother in the kitchen. We had a log rolling on our place, as was the custom in the country. After the work was over, the youngsters, while waiting for supper, engaged in some gymnastic exercises, trying the difficult feat of locking their heels over the back of their neck. Phillis observed these exercises, and the next day stole away up stairs to test her athletic capacity. After several unsuccessful attempts, she suddenly realized that her feet had forcibly gone over her head and were securely locked. Time and again Aunt Lucy, her mother, called and Phillis as often answered up stairs, but never came. Finally Aunt Lucy got her dander up, and picking up a switch started, saying, "Bound I fetch that gal down them stairs." Pretty soon there was a racket upstairs, and Aunt Lucy had worn out the switch before Phillis could explain that the witch had her.

The case of Anky, however, lends more zest to the witch's characteristic antipathy for the Negro. Mother had taken notice of the fact that Kate never made any demonstrations in the cabins, and conceived the reason why, accepting the witch's own statement. She exercised her genius and hit upon a scheme to outwit Kate, which was rather novel in its purpose. However, she turned the matter over in her own mind carefully, and spoke not a word about it, not even to father, for the reason, perhaps, that she was afraid of the thing, and believed she fared best by cultivating the regard it manifested for her; consequently no one knew a breath of her plans until the outcome of the scheme was developed.

Anky was a well-developed, buxom African girl, some eighteen years of age — a real Negro, so to speak, exuberant with that pungent aromatic which was so obnoxious to Kate's olfactory. Mother had determined to cautiously test her plan for getting rid of the witch, telling Anky, in her gentle patronizing way, that she wanted her for a house girl and desired that she should sleep in her room. The girl manifested some misgivings, but felt complimented by the distinction implied, and enquired of mother if she reckoned the old witch would not pester her? Being assured that there was not much danger, that Kate would be too busy entertaining the company to take any notice of her, her fears gave way to her plucked up courage and she followed mother's directions to the letter, keeping the whole matter a secret from the other Negroes and all the family until the test was made as to whether the witch would trouble her or not.

So one evening after supper Anky quietly slipped in the room with her pallet and spread it under mother's bed, fixing herself comfortably on it, to await the coming in of visitors and the witch and hear the talking. It was a high bedstead, with a white-fringed counterpane hanging to the floor, hiding Anky completely. She was delighted, and not a soul except mother knew she was there. Very soon the room was filled with visitors, keeping up a lively chit-chat while waiting the coming of Kate, and mother had taken a seat with the company anxiously waiting to see the outcome of her scheme.

Presently the voice of the witch angrily rang out above the din of conversation. with the exclamation, "There is a damn nigger in the house, it's Anky; I smell her under the bed and she's got to get out."

In an instant a noise was heard under the bed like that of a man clearing his throat, hawking and spitting vehemently, and Anky came rolling out like a log starting down hill, her face and head literally covered with foam like white spittle. She sprang to her feet with wonderful agility, frantically exclaiming, "Oh missus, missus, it's going to spit me to death. Let me out, let me out," and she went yelling all the way to the cabin, "Let me in, let me in."

The witch then addressed mother, "Say Luce, did you bring that nigger in here?"

"Yes," replied mother, "I told Anky that she might go under my bed, where she would be out of the way, to hear you talk and sing."

"I thought so," replied Kate, "I guess she heard me. Nobody but you, Luce, would have thought of such a smart trick as that, and if anybody else had done it I would have killed the damn nigger. Lord Jesus I won't get over that smell in a month!"

## The Mysterious Hand Shaking

The Johnson brothers, John and Calvin, perhaps had more intercourse with the witch than any other two men who visited our place during the excitement. That is they talked more with the invisible, entered more earnestly into the investigation by cultivating friendly and intimate relations. They were both very honorable men, of high standing in the community, but were very dissimilar in character. Calvin was a plain unassuming man of strict integrity, free from deception, faithful in everything he pretended, and would not swerve from the truth or break a promise knowingly and willfully under any circumstances. John was more dexterous, of a shrewd investigating turn of mind, guided by policy, and would make use of all legitimate means at hand to gain a point or accomplish a purpose, and he cultivated the witch more than any one else for the purpose of facilitating his investigations. Kate was very fond of gab, and John Johnson made use of every opportunity to engage the mage in conversation, hoping to draw out something that would give a clue to the mystery, but it appears that all of his wits were baffled, and that the seer was all the while aware of his purpose. The question arose as to the character of the blows received by so many persons on the cheek after retiring. The sound was like a slap of an open hand, and everyone to testified that it left a sting like that of a hand, even to the prints of the fingers being felt. Calvin Johnson conceived the idea of asking the witch to shake hands with him. After much persuasion Kate agreed to comply with the request, on one condition, that Calvin would first promise not to try to grasp or hold the hand that would be laid in his. This he agreed to, and then holding out his hand, in an instant he felt the pressure of the invisible. Mr. Johnson testified that he felt it very sensibly, and that the touch was soft and delicate like the hand of a lady, and no one ever doubted his statement. John Johnson begged Kate to shake hands with him, persisting that he was as good a friend as his brother, but the witch refused, telling John "No, you only want a chance to catch me." John vowed that he would not attempt anything of the kind. Kate still refused, replying, "I know you, Jack Johnson; you are a grand rascal, trying to find me out, and I won't trust you." Two or three other persons claimed to have shaken hands with the witch, which I don't know about, though many testified to the force of the hand as felt on the cheek.

## He Stole His Wife

It was not uncommon for Kate to recognize strangers the moment they entered the house, speaking to them on familiar terms. Here is one instance I will note. Four strangers who had traveled a long distance (whose names I cannot now remember, there were so many unknown callers), arrived late — on a dark night, and knocking at the door, and were admitted. They were unknown to any one in the house or on the place, but the moment they entered the door, and before they could speak to introduce themselves, Kate announced one by name, exclaiming, "He is the grand rascal who stole his wife. He pulled her out of her father's house through a window, and hurt her arm, making her cry; then he whispered to her, 'Hush honey don't cry, it will soon get well.'" The strangers were greatly confused. They stood dumbfounded, pausing some time before they could speak. The gentleman was asked before leaving if the witch had stated the facts in regard to his matrimonial escapade. He said yes, the circumstance occurred just as stated.

## Detective Williams

A good looking stranger arrived who introduced himself as Mr. Williams, a professional detective, stating that he had heard much of the witch mystery, which no one could explain, and having considerable experience in unraveling tangled affairs and mysteries, he had traveled a long dist ance for the purpose of investigating this matter, if he should be permitted to do so; further stating that he did not believe in either preternatural or supernatural things, and professed to be an expert in detecting jugglery, sleight-of-hand performances, illusions, etc., and would certainly expose these manifestations, so much talked of if given a fair chance. Father bid the gentleman a hearty welcome, telling him that he was just the man that was wanted. "Make my house your home, and make free with everything here as if your own, as long as you think proper to stay," said father, and Mr. Williams politely accepted the invitation and hung up his hat. Mr. Williams was rather a portly, strong-muscled, well dressed, handsome gentleman. He was no less self-possessed, and wise in his own conceit, full of gab, letting his tongue run continually, detailing to the company his wonderful exploits in the detective business, and was very sure he would bring Kate to grief before leaving. A day and night passed and Kate, for some cause best known to the witch, kept silent, making no show except a little scratching on the walls and thumping about the room, just enough to let the company know that the spirit was present. Mr. Williams became very impatient, appearing disgruntled, and spoke his mind more freely. He said to a coterie of gentlemen who were discussing the witch, that he was convinced that the whole thing was a family affair, an invention gotten up for a sensation to draw people and make money, and the actors were afraid to make any demonstrations while he was present, knowing his profession and business, and that he would most assuredly expose the trick. One of the gentlemen told father what Williams had said, and it made him very indignant. He felt outraged that such a charge should be made without the evidence, by a man professing to be a gentleman, to whom he had extended every courtesy and hospitality, and had proffered any assistance he might call for, and in a rage he threatened to order Williams from the place immediately. Just at this juncture Kate spoke, "No you don't, old Jack, let him stay; I will attend to the gentleman and satisfy him that he is not so smart as he thinks." Father said no more, nor did he take any action in the matter, but treated Mr. Williams gentlemanly as he did the others, nor was anything more heard from Kate. The house was crowded with visitors that night, all expectantly and anxious to hear the witch talk, and sat till late bed time awaiting the sound of the mystifying voice, but not a word or single demonstration of any kind was heard from Kate. This confirmed the detective in his conjectures, and he repeated to several visitors his conclusions, declaring that the witch would not appear again as long as he remained. After they were all tired out, mother had straw mattresses spread over the floor to accommodate the company. Mr. Williams, being the largest gentleman present, selected one of these pallets to himself. All retired and the light was extinguished, and a night of quiet rest was promising. As soon as perfect quiet prevailed, and everyone appeared to be in a dose of sleep, Mr. Williams found himself pinioned, as it were, to the floor by some irresistible force from which he was utterly powerless to extricate himself, stout as he was, and the witch scratching and pounding him with vengeance. He yelled out to the top of his voice calling for help and mercy. Kate held up long enough to inquire of the detective, which one of the family he thought had him, and then let in again, giving him an unmerciful beating, while the man plead for life. All of this occurred in less than two minutes, and before a candle could be lighted, and as soon as the light appeared the pounding ceased, but Kate did a good deal of talking, more than Mr. Williams cared to hear. The detective was badly used up and the worst scared man that ever came to our house. He sat up on a chair the balance of the night, with a burning candle by his side, subjected to the witch's tantalizing sarcasm, ridicule and derision, questioning him as to which of the family was carrying on the devilment, how he liked the result of his investigations, how long he intended to stay, etc. As soon as day dawned, Mr. Williams ordered his horse, and could not be prevailed upon to remain until after breakfast.

## Kate Gets in Bed With William Porter

William Porter was a very prominent citizen of the community, a gentleman of high integrity, regarded for his strict veracity. He was also a good friend to our family, and spent many nights with us during the trouble, taking his turn with others in entertaining Kate, which was necessary to have any peace at all, and also agreeable to those of an investigating turn of mind who were not afraid, and this was Mr. Porter's character; like John Johnson, he rather cultivated the spirit, and said he was fond of gabbing with Kate. This seemed to please the witch, and they got along on good terms. William Porter was at this time a bachelor, occupying his house alone. The building was a large hewn log house, with a partition dividing it into two rooms. There was one chimney having a very large fireplace, and the other end was used for a bedroom — entered by a door in the partition. I give this as related by Mr. Porter himself, to a large company at Father's, and as he has often repeated the same to many persons, and no one doubted his truthfulness. Said he:

"It was a cold night and I made a big log fire before retiring to keep the house warm. As soon as I got in bed I heard scratching and thumping about the bed, just like Kate's tricks, as I thought, but was not long in doubt as to the fact. Presently I felt the cover drawling to the backside, and immediately the witch spoke, when I recognized the unmistakable voice of Kate. 'Billy, I have come to sleep with you and keep you warm.' I replied, 'Well Kate if you are going to sleep with me, you must behave yourself.' I clung to the cover, feeling that it was drawing from me, as it appeared to be raised from the bed on the other side, and something snake-like crawling under. I was never afraid of the witch, or apprehended that it would do me any harm but somehow this produced a kind of chilly sensation that was simply awful. The cover continued to slip in spite of my tenacious grasp, and was twisted into a roll on the back side of the bed, just like a boy would roll himself in a quilt, and not a strip was left on me. I jumped out of bed in a second, and observing that Kate had rolled up in the cover, the thought struck me, 'I have got you now, you rascal, and will burn you up.' In an instant I grabbed the roll of cover in my arms and started to the fire, intending to throw the cover, witch and all in the blaze. I discovered that it was very weighty, and smelt awful. I had not gone half way across the room before the luggage got so heavy and became so offensive that I was compelled to drop it on the floor and rush out of doors for a breath of fresh air. The odor emitted from the roll was the most offensive stench I ever smelt. It was absolutely stifling and I could not have endured it another second. After being refreshed I returned to the room, and gathered up the roll of bed clothing shook them out, but Kate had departed, and there was no unusual weight or offensive odor remaining, and this is just how near I came catching the witch."

## Our School Day Experience

Major Garaldus Pickering, who was a distinguished man of that day, kept a large school near by, which Joel and myself attended, and had many little experiences with Kate along the way. The custom was to take in school as soon as the teacher could get there, a little after sunrise, and dismiss about thirty minutes before sunset. Our route was through the woods, and some briar patches and hazel thickets by the wayside. Passing these thickets, returning home, sticks of wood and rocks were often tossed at us, but never with much force, and we soon learned not to fear any harm from this pastime, and frequently cut notches on the sticks, casting them back into the thicket from whence they came, and invariably the same sticks would be hurled back at us. After night Kate would recount everything that occurred along the way. Even if one of us stumped a toe, falling over, the witch claimed to have caused it, and would describe how it appeared in the form of a rabbit or something else at certain places. Our most serious trouble, however, was experienced at home, the witch continually pulling the cover off, and twisting our hair, and it was hard for a tired boy to get any sleep.

## Joel Severely Whipped

It happened that Joel and myself were left to occupy a room alone one night, and were troubled less than usual in the early part of the night, but Kate put in good time just before day. It was quite a cold morning, and rather too early to get up, but Kate continued pulling the cover off and jerking my hair, and I got out of bed and dressed myself. Joel, however, was much vexed, and said some ugly things about "Old Kate," and gathering up the cover from the floor, he rolled himself up in it for another nap. Directly the witch snatched it from him again. Joel became enraged, pulling at the cover while Kate seemed to be hawking and spitting in his face, and he had to turn loose the cover. This made Joel raving mad, and he laid flat on his back, kicking with all his might, calling old Kate the meanest kind of names. "Go away from here, you nasty old thing," he exclaimed. Kate became furious also, exclaiming, "You little rascal, I'll let you know who you are talking to." That moment Joel felt the blows falling fast and heavy, and no boy ever received such a spanking as he got that morning, and he never forgot it. It was absolutely frightful. I could do nothing for his relief. He yelled frantically with all of his might, arousing the whole house, nor did his punisher cease spanking until father entered the door with a light, finding him almost lifeless. The blows sounded like the spanking of an open heavy hand, and certainly there was no one in the room but Joel and myself, and if there had been, there was no way of escaping except by the door which father entered, and that would have been impossible unobserved.

## Chasing the Shakers

The Shakertown People at that time kept their trading men on the road continually, traveling through the country, dealing with the people. They went in two's, generally on horseback, and could be distinguished from other people at a distance by their broad brim hats and peculiarity in dress. The two who traveled through our section always made it convenient to call at our house for dinner or a night's lodging. It was about the regular time for these gentlemen to come around, and near the dinner hour one of the servants came in announcing to mother that the Shakers were coming down the lane. This was a notice to increase the contents of the dinner Pot.

ate spoke up immediately, exclaiming, "Them damn Shakers

shan't stop this time." Father was troubled a good deal by breachy [sic] stock on the outside pushing the fences down, and generally sent Harry, a Negro boy, around every day to drive away stock and see that the fences were up. There were three large dogs on the place that the boy always carried along, and he had them well trained and always eager for a chase, and would start at his call, yelping furiously. Harry was nowhere about. He was out on the farm with the other hands. But instantly after Kate spoke Harry's voice was heard in the front yard calling the dogs, "Here Caesar, here Tiger, here Bulger, here, here, sic, sic," slapping his hands. Not a soul but the Shakers coming down the lane could be seen. The dogs, however, responded with savage yelping, going in a fury, following the voice that left the way egging them on, and just as the Shakers were nearing the turning in gate, the dogs leaped the fence at their horses' heels, and Harry's voice was there too, hollering, "Sic, sic, take 'em." The Shakers put whip to their horses and the dogs after them, and Kate vehemently aging the dogs on and hilariously enjoying the sport. It was a lively chase, and broke the Shakers from coming that way again. The witch enjoyed the sport greatly, laughing and repeating the affair to visitors, injecting many funny expressions in describing the chase, and how the Shakers held on to their big hats.

### Mother Bell's Illness — The Witch Sings Sweet Songs and Brings Her Hazelnuts and Grapes

The story of the hazelnuts and grapes brought to mother during her illness was hard for many to believe, and it may prove a severe strain on the credulity of the reader, but it is nevertheless true, and will be verified by several worthy persons who witnessed the facts and have stated the same to many people. Kate had all along manifested a high regard for mother, often remarking, "Old Luce is a good woman." This was very gratifying to the family; we were all much devoted to her, and this earnest expression of tender respect for her; so often repeated, was to a great extent an assurance that whatever might befall other members of the family, mother would be spared personal affliction. She was fearful of the thing, and could not see any good sense or policy in antagonizing what was now evidently a powerful, intelligent and incomprehensible agency, and therefore she conceived it to be the best policy to cultivate the kind manifestations of the witch, and she exercised all the gentleness of her nature toward Kate, as she did her tender affections for her children. This proved to be the best policy, for it is evident that she appeased the seer's malice in many instances, except in father's case, toward whom the malignity was unrelenting and beyond control.

About the middle of September, 1820, mother was taken down with a spell of pleurisy, and then it was that Kate manifested a sorrowful nature, growing more plaintive every day as the disease progressed, giving utterance to woeful expressions that were full of touching sympathy. "Luce, poor Luce, I am so sorry you are sick. Don't you feel better, Luce? What can I do for you, Luce?"

These and many other expressions of sympathy and anxious inquiries were given vent by the saddened voice, that now appeared to remain constantly in mother's room prattling all through the day, changing to a more joyful tone when she indicated any temporary relief. The persistent jabbering and disquietude was enough to craze a well person, but mother bore it all patiently, frequently replying to questions.

Sometimes she would reply, "Oh Kate, I am too sick to talk to you." Then the voice would hush for some time, as if choking expression.

When anything was wanted or called for that was needed for mother's comfort, the witch would speak promptly, telling precisely where the article could be found. And so the strange voice continued from day to day, mystifying everyone who came to visit and minister to mother's wants, and it was utterly impossible to distinguish from whence it came, and yet so pathetic as to affect the sympathy of everyone who came within hearing.

It was noticeable also that Kate kept quiet when mother was apparently at rest or sleeping. She rested better in the latter part of the night, and was somewhat refreshed for the morning, and as soon as she was aroused Kate was heard inquiring, "How do you feel this morning, Luce? Did you rest well through the night? Don't you want to hear a song, Luce?"

Mother was very fond of vocal music, in which Kate excelled, and it was her pleasure to reply, "Yes Kate, sing something sweet."

While the witch sung a number of beautiful stanzas, the following was the favorite, which was sung every day:

> Come my heart and let us try
> For a little season
> Every burden to lay by
> Come and let us reason.

> What is this that casts you down?
> Who are those that grieve you?

*Speak and let the worst be known,*
  *Speaking may relieve you.*

*Christ by faith I sometimes see*
  *And He doth relieve me,*
*But my fears return again,*
  *These are they that grieve me.*

*Troubled like the restless Sea,*
  *Feeble, faint and fearful,*
*Plagued with every sore disease,*
  *How can I be cheerful?*

No rhythmical sound or melody ever fell upon the ear with sweeter pathos, coming as it did like a volume of symphony from a bursting heart. I have seen the tears trickle down mother's fevered cheeks, while friends would turn away to hide repressed weeping. Sick as she was, mother never neglected to compliment the song. "Thank you Kate, that was so sweet and beautiful, it makes me feel better," which the witch seemed to appreciate. Mother gradually grew worse, the disease reaching a serious stage. The doctor was still very hopeful, but the family and our good neighbors were feeling the deepest concern. Father became very restless and apprehensive of the worst. Her appetite failed entirely, and this distressed Kate woefully. The neighbors brought all sorts of tempting good things to induce her to eat, and this example the observing witch imitated, conceiving the idea, no doubt, that the most important thing was the discovery of something agreeable to her appetite, and this was the circumstance that seemed to have inspired the action of the witch in bringing the nuts and grapes. Wild fruits were plentiful in the bottoms and woods around the place, and were then ripening. Tim first instance was the appearance of the hazelnuts. The same plaintive voice was heard exclaiming, "Luce, poor Luce, how do you feel now? Hold out your hands, Luce, and I will give you something." Mother stretched her arms, holding her hands together open, and the hazelnuts were dropped from above into her hands. This was witnessed by several ladies who had called in to see mother, and it was so incredible that the floor above was examined to see if there was not a loose plank or some kind of opening through which they were dropped, hut it was found to be perfectly secure, and not even a crevice through which a pin could pass. After some time the amazement was increased by the same voice inquiring, "Say Luce, why don't you eat the hazelnuts?" Mother replied that she could not crack them. Then the exclamation, "Well

I will crack some for you," and instantly the sound of the cracking was heard, and the cracked nuts dropped on her bed within hand's reach, and the same passionate voice continued insisting on mother's eating the nuts, that they would do her good. Next came the grapes in the same way, the voice importuning her to eat them, that they would do her good. Mother was thoughtful in expressing her thanks, remarking, "You are so kind, Kate, but I am too sick to eat them." From this time on mother steadily improved, coming out of a severe spell that held her down some twenty days, and no one could express more joy and gladness than Kate, who also praised Dr. Hopson, the good physician who brought her through safely. As soon as mother was convalescent, Kate devoted more attention to the entertainment of the large number of visitors who were constantly coming to hear the mysterious voice. One evening the room was full of company, all deeply interested in discussing the phenomena of the grapes, etc., when the presence of the witch was announced by the voice exclaiming, "Who wants some grapes?" and before any one could answer, a large bunch of luscious wild grapes fell out on Elizabeth's lap. The bunch was passed around and all tasted of the fruit, and were satisfied that it was no illusion. Kate evinced remarkable knowledge of the forest, and would tell us where to find plenty of grapes, hazelnuts, herbs of every kind, good hickory for axe handles, or tough sticks for a maul.

## Mrs. Martha Bell's Stockings

Kate, as before intimated, visited the family of Brother Jesse Bell quite often, making demonstrations, but never to the extent of the manifestations at home. Jesse's wife, whom the witch called "Pots," observed mother's policy in humoring the warlock, paying kindly attention to its gabble, incurring favor or kindly relations, and she too was treated with such consideration as to relieve her fears of any immediate harm. Jesse Bell and Bennett Porter had determined to move with their families to Panola county, Mississippi, and were shaping their affairs to that end, as soon as circumstances would admit. This phenomena I give as related by Martha herself, there being no other witnesses to the circumstance, but I can not doubt her statement, which is borne out by other facts. Late in the afternoon she was sitting out some ten steps on the east side in the shade of the house, engaged in pealing apples for drying. She heard a kind of buzzing or indistinct whispering in her ear, and recognized at once that it was the voice of the witch, and spoke to it, inquiring, "What do you want, Kate? Speak out so I can understand you."

Then the witch spoke plainly, saying, "Pots, I have brought you a present to keep in remembrance of me when you go to your far away new home. Will you accept it?" She replied, "Certainly Kate, I will gladly accept any present you may bring. What is it?" Just then a small roll, neatly wrapped in paper, fell on her lap. She looked up and around in every direction, but no one was near, nor could she discover from whence it came. In her confusion the witch spoke again, saying, "I brought it, Pots; see what a nice pair of stockings. I want you to keep them for your burial, to remember me, and never wear them." She then stripped off the paper and found a pair of elegant black silk hose, for which she thanked Kate, promising to keep them as requested. Martha said she discovered an ugly splotch on one of the hose, which she was eyeing with much curiosity, when the witch spoke very promptly, remarking, "That is blood. They killed a beef at Kate Batts' this morning, and the blood spattered on the stocking." Martha said she was so disconcerted and perplexed that she could not speak, and Kate departed, or said nothing more. Jesse Bell came in from the field very soon, and when made acquainted with all the facts as above stated, determined to go at once to the Batts home and ascertain the facts regarding the witch's story of the butchering that morning. He did not mention the circumstance, but very soon Mrs. Batts expressed herself as very glad that he had called, stating that they had killed a fine young beef that morning, and intended sending Patsy (his wife) a piece, but had had no opportunity, and wished him to take it, which he did. So this part of the witch's story was confirmed, and Jesse further ascertained from Mrs. Batts that it had been a very busy day, and not one of the family had left the place during the day, or but for the pressing engagement she would have sent the beef to his house. Moreover, Martha Bell had not left the premises, nor had any visitor been on the place.

## Dr. Mize, the Wizard

During the period of these exciting demonstrations, ever so many detectives, wise men, witch doctors, or conjurers, came to exercise their skill on Kate, and were permitted to practice schemes and magic arts to their heart's content, and all were brought to grief in some way, confessing that the phenomena was something beyond comprehension. One notable instance was that of Dr. Mize, of Simpson County, Ky., some thirty-five miles away, whose fame as a magician had been widely spread, and many brought word to father of his genius, urging him to send for the noted conjurer. The truth is, father had become alarmed about his own condition. His spells of contortions of the face, twitching of the flesh and stiffness of the tongue, were gradually growing more frequent and severe. His friends observed this, and also that the animosity of the witch toward him was increasing in vehemence, every word spoken to him being a blast of calumnious aspersions, and threatenings of some dire evil which was horrifying. He had also become convinced from his observations, that this terrible thing had the power, as it claimed, to so afflict him, and that the purpose was to torture his life out, as it also declared; and under these circumstances he yielded to the many persuasions to exhaust all means and efforts to free himself and family from the pestilence. He consulted with Mr. James Johnson about the matter, who thought it would be well to give Dr. Mize a trial, and farther proposed to go with Drew after the famous wizard. So it was agreed that Mr. Johnson and Drew were to start on the hunt for Dr. Mize after three o'clock in the morning, while Kate was not about, and clear the neighborhood before the morning hour for the witch's appearance. The whole matter was to be kept a profound secret, and no one was let into the understanding. Drew made ready to accompany Mr. Johnson on a business trip, to be absent two or three days, and that was all that was known about it. They got off according to the arrangement in good time, and had perhaps passed Springfield before day. Kate came as usual that morning, observing first Drew's absence, setting up an anxious inquiry for him. Not one of the family could give any information concerning him, and the witch seemed baffled and disappeared, and was not heard again during the day, but returned that night in great glee, having discovered the whole secret, telling all about Drew and Mr. Johnson's trip. Kate went on to say, "I got on their track and overtook them twenty miles on the way, and followed along some distance, and when I hopped in the road before them, looking like a poor old sick rabbit, 'Old Sugar Mouth' said, 'There is your witch, Drew; take her up in your lap. Don't you see how tired she is?'" Kate continued to gossip about the trip in a hilarious way, manifesting much satisfaction in discovering the deep laid scheme, but no one knew how true the story was until Mr. Johnson and Drew returned the following evening, when they confirmed everything that Kate had stated. Mr. Johnson said that he did not really believe at the time of calling Drew's attention to the rabbit, that it was the witch, but spoke of its peculiar action in a jocular way, as a mere matter of pastime, nor did Drew think otherwise of it. They found Dr. Mize at his home east of Franklin, Ky., told him the story of our trouble, and the information received concerning his power to dispel witchery, etc. The Doctor said it was out of the ordinary line of phenomena, but he had no doubt of his ability to remove the spell and expose the craft that had brought it on, and he set the time, some ten days ahead, when he would be ready to begin the experiment. Accordingly, the wise man put in his appearance, having studied the question, and was prepared for business, making boasts of his knowledge of spirits and skill in casting out devils, much to the disgust of father, who had about sized him up on sight. However, like others, Mize was treated courteously and allowed to pursue his own plans. The wizard stayed three or four days, hearing not a breath from Kate. In the meanwhile he found an old shotgun that had been out of repair some time, and he at once discovered that the witch had put a spell on it. He soon cleaned the old gun, readjusted the lock and trigger, performed some conjurations, making the gun shoot as well as ever. This much, taken in consideration with the fact that the witch had kept perfectly quiet since his arrival, he considered as remarkable progress, and he doubted the return of Kate. Certain he was that the witch would hardly show up as long as he remained; witches, he said, were always shy of him. So Mize continued, working sorcery, making curious mixtures, performing incantations, etc., to the amusement of those who observed his actions. Finally Kate put in, questioning the conjurer impertinently as to what he was doing, and the object of his sorcery. Mize was nonplussed by the mysterious voice, which he had not before heard, recognizing that the witch had come to keep company with him. He tried to be reticent and evasive, intimating that a witch had no business prying into his affairs. Kate, however, continued to ply him with hard questions, and finally suggested to Dr. Mize that he had omitted some very important ingredients for his charm mixture. "What is that?" inquired Mize with astonishment. "If you were a witch doctor you would know how to aerify that mess, so as to pass into the aeriform state, and see the spirit that talks to you, without asking silly questions," replied Kate. "What do you know about this business, anyhow?" again inquired the bewildered conjurer. Kate then told him that he was an old fool and didn't know what he was doing, and then started in to cursing Mize like blue blazes. Such a string of blasting oaths was never heard, and Dr. Mize was frightened out of his wits, and was anxious to get away. "That thing," he said, knew so much more about witchcraft than he did, that he could do nothing with it.

Mize arranged for an early start home the next morning. Somehow his horse refused to go off kindly, rearing and kicking up. Finally Kate came to the rescue, proposing to make the horse go, and accompany the Doctor home. Immediately the horse started with a rush, kicking and snorting, and went off at full speed with the Doctor hanging on to the mane. The witch came that night in great glee, describing the trip home with the "old fraud," and the tricks played on him along the way, just as Mize described the affair to his neighbors.

## The Doubles or Apparitions

Much has been talked about Bennett Porter shooting at the witch. Porter, according to his own statement, did shoot at an object that appeared to his wife and Elizabeth, as described by them, but saw nothing himself, except the bent saplings in motion. This circumstance occurred during the time the witch family appeared on scene. Elizabeth was there on a visit to her sister. Bennett Porter was absent during the day, filling an engagement at Fort's mill, which was in course of construction, and returned home late in the afternoon. The hens were laying about the stables, which were located on the opposite side of the lane from the house. Esther started across the lane that afternoon to gather up the eggs. Just as she passed from the yard into road, she observed a woman walking slowly up the lane toward the house, and she hurried on her mission and returned just in time to meet the lady at the front entrance. She recognized the person as one of her neighbors, and spoke to her pleasantly, to which the woman made no reply. She repeated the salutation, which again failed to elicit any response. The woman appeared to have taken off her bonnet and let her hair down, and was engaged in combing out her hair as she walked, and stopped just opposite the house, where Esther met her, continuing the combing, and appeared deeply absorbed or troubled. Esther said she invited the lady in the house, repeating the solicitation several times, to which the woman paid no attention. She felt much chagrined by the strange conduct of her neighbor, and concluded that something was wrong with the lady or that she had become offended towards her, and she passed in, leaving the woman standing in the lane, combing her hair. She called Elizabeth's attention to the woman and her conduct, and they both observed her still in the same attitude. Presently she climbed on the yard fence, sitting there some five minutes, still combing her hair, and then she tucked it up in the usual way and left the fence, crossing over into the stable lot, where she could not have possibly had any business. The lot enclosed some three or four acres, a grove mostly of young saplings on the further side, ill the midst of which was a large knotty log. The woman walked across the lot, passing around the log, when there appeared three other persons, two younger women or girls, and a boy. Each one bent down a sapling, sitting upon them and riding up and down, giving motion to the spring afforded by the bush. While this exercise still continued, Bennett Porter returned home, finding Esther and Elisabeth excited over the strange demonstrations that they tried to point out to him. He said he could see the bushes in motion, but could not see the persons described. He suggested that they were the witch apparitions, and got his gun, insisting that Esther should shoot at one of the objects. While he was getting his rifle, the appearances let the saplings up and took positions behind the log, first one and then another showing a head above the log. Esther refused to shoot, but directed Porter to shoot near a large knot on the log, where one of the heads appeared. He fired and his bullet cut the bark on the log just where he aimed, but nothing more was seen of the four persons, nor could they, as Porter thought, have escaped from the lot without detection. They all three went to the log, and searched the lot over, and could discover no signs except the bent saplings, and the mark of the bullet on the log. Now whether these were doubles, apparitions, witches, or real persons, the witch family in their carousal that night made much ado about it, declaring to the company present that Bennett Porter had shot at Jerusalem and had broken his arm with the bullet.

## The Poisonous Vial — The Last Illness and Death of John Bell, Sr.

I have already written more about this abomination than contemplated in the outset, and still have not told the half; but have presented enough, to which others can testify, to enable the reader to form some idea of the heinous thing, and the horrors that our family had to endure during the early settlement of Robertson county, from an unknown enemy, and for an unknown cause. Whether it was witchery, such as afflicted people in past centuries and the darker ages, whether some gifted fiend of hellish nature, practicing sorcery for selfish enjoyment, or some more modern science akin to that of mesmerism, or some hobgoblin native to the wilds of the country, or a disembodied soul shut out from heaven, or an evil spirit like those Paul drove out of the man into the swine, setting them mad; or a demon let loose from hell, I am unable to decide; nor has any one yet divined its nature or cause for appearing, and I trust this description of the monster in all forms and shapes, and of many tongues, will lead experts who may come with a wiser generation, to a correct conclusion and satisfactory explanation.

However, no part of what I have written would be complete without the finale; the climax which I now approach with a shudder that fills my frame with horror, bringing fresh to memory scenes and events that chilled the blood in my young veins, cheating me out of twenty years of life. It hangs over me like the pall of death, and sends weary thoughts like fleeting shadows through my brain, reviving in memory those demoniac shrieks that came so oft from an invisible and mysterious source, rending the air with vile and hideous curses that drove me frantic with fear. It is no ghastly dream of a fevered brain that comes to haunt one's thoughts, but a sad, fearful reality, a tremendous truth, that thrills the heart with an unspeakable fear that no word painting can portray on paper. Courageous men in battle line may rush upon bristling bayonets and blazing musketry, and face the roaring cannon's month, because they can see the enemy and know who and what they are fighting; but when it comes to meeting an unknown enemy of demonstrative power, with gall upon its tongue and venom in its bosom, heaving bitter curses and breathing threats of dire consequences, which one knows not of, nor can judge in what shape or form the calamity is to come, the stoutest heart will prove a coward, faltering and quivering with painful fear. Why should my father, John Bell, be inflicted with such a terrible curse? Why should such a fate befall a man striving to live uprightly? I would be untrue to myself and my parentage, should I fail to state boldly that John Bell was a man every inch of him and in every sense of the term. No man was ever more faithful and swift in the discharge of every duty, to his family, to the church, to his neighbor's, to his fellow man, and to his God, in the fullness of his capacity and that faith which led him to love and accept Christ as a Savior. No mortal man ever brought a charge of delinquency or dishonor to his door. Not even the ghastly fiend that haunted him to his death, in all of its vile curses and evil threats, ever brought an accusation against him, or uttered a solitary word that reflected upon his honor, his character, his courage, or his integrity. He lived in peace, and in the enjoyment of the full confidence of his neighbors, and lacked not for scores of friends in his severest trials. Then why this affliction? Where the cause? Which no man, saint, angel from heaven, or demon from hell, has ever assigned. If there was any hidden or unknown cause why he should have thus suffered, or if it was in the providence of God a natural consequence, then why should the torments of a demon have been visited upon Elizabeth, who was a girl of tender years, brought up under the careful training of a Christian mother, and was free from guile and the wiles of the wicked world, and innocent of all offense? Yet this vile, heinous, unknown devil, torturer of human flesh, that preyed upon the fears of people like a ravenous vulture, spared not her, but rather chose her as a shining mark for an exhibition of its wicked stratagems and devilish tortures. And never did it cease to practice upon her fears, insult her modesty, stick pins in her body, pinching and bruising her flesh, slapping her cheeks, disheveling and tangling her hair, tormenting her in many ways, until she surrendered that most cherished hope which animates every young heart. Was this the stratagem of a human genius skilled in the black art; was it an enchantment, a freak in destiny, or the natural consequence of disobedience to some law in nature? Let a wiser head than mine answer and explain the mystery. Another problem in the development of these mysterious manifestations, that has always puz zled my understanding: Why should the husband and father, the head of the family, and the daughter, the pet and pride of the household, the centre of all family affections, be selected to bear the invectives of this terrible visitation, while demonstrations of the tenderest love from the same source was bestowed upon the wife and mother? If it was a living, intelligent creature, what could have been the dominating faculty of its nature, which made this discrimination? Could it have been an intelligent human devotion springing from an emotional nature that could so love the wife and mother, and cherish such bitter enmity for her husband and offspring, both of whom she loved most devotedly? I think not; only a fiend of a hellish nature, with poisoned blood and seared conscience, if a conscience at all, could have possessed such attributes. Yet we, who experienced or witnessed the demonstration, know that there was a wonderful power of intelligence, possessing knowledge of men and things, a spirit of divination, that could read minds, tell men's secrets, quote the Scriptures, repeat sermons, sing hymns and songs, assume bodily forms, and with all, an immense physical force behind the manifestations.

Father continued to suffer with spells as I have already described, the jerking and twitching of his face, and the swelling of his tongue, fearfully distorting his whole physiogamy. These spells would last from one to two days, and after passing off, he would be up and about his business, apparently in strong robust health. As time advanced the spells grew more frequent and severe, and there was no periodical time for their return, and along toward the last I stayed with him all the time, especially when he left the house, going with him wherever he went. The witch also grew more angry and virulent in disposition. Every word uttered to "Old Jack" was a blast of curses and heinous threats, while to mother, "Old Luce," it continued most tender, loving and kind. About the middle of October father had a very severe attack, which kept him confined to the house six or eight days. The witch cursed and raved like a maniac for several days, and ceased not from troubling him. However, he temporarily overcame this attack, and was soon able to be out, though he would not venture far from the house. But it was not destined that he should enjoy a long respite. After a week's recuperation he felt much stronger, and called me very early one morning to go with him to the hog pen, some three hundred yards from the house, for the purpose of giving directions in separating the porkers intended for fattening from the stock hogs. We had not gone far before one of his shoes was jerked off. I replaced it on his foot, drawing the strings tight, tying a double hard knot. After going a few steps farther, the other shoe flew off in the same manner, which was replaced and tied as in the case of the first.

In no way that I could tie them would they hold, notwithstanding his shoes fitted close and were a little hard to put on, and we were walking over a smooth, dry road. This worried him prodigiously; nevertheless, he bore up strongly, and after much delay and worry we reached the place, and he gave directions, seeing the hogs properly separated as he desired, and the hands left for other work, and we started back for the house.

We had not gone many steps before his shoes commenced jerking off as before, and presently he complained of a blow on his face, which felt like an open hand, that almost stunned him, and he sat down on a log that lay by the road side. Then his face commenced jerking with fearful contortions, soon his whole body, and then his shoes would fly off as fast as I could put them on. The situation was trying and made me shudder. I was terrified by the spectacle of the contortions that seized father, as if to convert him into a very demon to swallow me up.

Having finished tying father's shoes, I raised myself up to hear the reviling sound of derisive songs piercing the air with terrorizing force. As the demoniac shrieks died away in triumphant rejoicing, the spell passed off, and I saw the tears chasing down father's yet quivering cheeks. The trace of faltering courage marked every lineament of his face with a wearied expression of fading hope.

He turned to me with an expression of tender, compassionate fatherly devotion, exclaiming in a woeful passionate tone, "Oh my son, my son, not long will you have a father to wait on so patiently. I cannot much longer survive the persecutions of this terrible thing. It is killing me by slow tortures, and I feel that the end is nigh."

This expression sent a pang to my bosom which I had never felt before. Mingled sorrow and terror took possession of me and sent a tremor through my frame that I can never forget. If the earth could have opened and swallowed us up, it would have been a joyful deliverance. My heart bleeds now at every pore as I pen these lines, refreshing my memory with thoughts of the terror that possessed me then in anticipation of a fearful tragedy that might be enacted before father could move from his position.

That moment he turned his eyes upward and lifted his soul to heaven in a burst of fervent passionate prayer, such as I had never heard him utter before. He prayed the Lord that if it were possible, to let this terrible affliction pass. He beseeched God to forsake him not in the trying ordeal, but to give him courage to meet this unknown devastating enemy in the trying emergency, and faith to lift him to the confidence and love of a blessed Savior, and with all to relieve his family and loved ones from the terrible afflictions of this wicked, unknown, terrifying, blasphemous agency. It was in this strain that father prayed, pouring out his soul in a passionate force that seemed to take hold of Christ by a powerful faith that afforded fresh courage and renewed strength. After he had finished his prayer, a feeling of calmness and reconciliation seemed to possess him, and he appeared to have recovered from the severe shock. The reviling songster had disappeared, and he rose up remarking that he felt better and believed he could walk to the house, and he did, meeting with no more annoyance as we proceeded on the way.

However, he took to his bed immediately on arriving at the house, and though able to be up and down for several weeks, he never left the house again, and seemed all the while perfectly reconciled to the terrible fate that awaited him. He gradually declined; nothing that friends could do brought any relief. Mother was almost constantly at his bedside with all the devotion of her nature. Brother John attended closely in the room, ministering to him, and good neighbors were in constant attendance. The witch was carrying on its deviltry more or less all the while.

The crisis, however, came on the morning of December 19th. Father, sick as he was, had not up to this time failed to awake at his regular hour, according to his long custom, and arouse the family. That morning he appeared to be sleeping so soundly, mother quietly slipped, out of the room to superintend breakfast, while brothers John and Drew looked after the farm hands and feeding the stock, and would not allow him to be disturbed until after breakfast.

Noticing then that he was sleeping unnaturally, it was thought best to awaken him, when it was discovered that he was in a deep stupor, and could not be aroused to any sensibility. Brother John attended to giving him medicine, and went immediately to the cupboard where he had carefully put away the medicines prescribed for him, but instead he found a smoky looking vial, which was about one-third full of dark colored liquid. He set up an inquiry at once to know who had moved the medicine, and no one had touched it, and neither could any one on the place give any account of the vial. Dr. George Hopson, of Port Royal, was sent for in great haste and soon arrived; also neighbors John Johnson, Alex Gunn and Frank Miles arrived early, and were there when the vial was found.

Kate, the witch, in the meantime broke out with joyous exultation, exclaiming, "It's useless for you to try to relieve Old Jack, I have got him this time; he will never get up from that bed again." Kate was then asked about the vial of medicine found in the cupboard, and replied, "I put it there, and gave Old Jack a big dose out of it last night while he was asleep, which fixed him."

This was all the information that could be drawn from the witch or any other source concerning the vial of medicine. Certain it was that no member of the family ever saw it before, or could tell anything about it. In fact no vial and no medicine of any kind had been brought to the house by any one else except by Dr. Hopson, and then it was handled carefully.

Dr. Hopson, on arrival, examined the vial and said he did not leave it, and could not tell what it contained. It was then suggested that the contents be tested on something. Alex Gunn caught a cat, and Brother John run a straw into the vial and drew it through the cat's mouth, wiping the straw on its tongue. The cat jumped and whirled over a few times, stretched out, kicked, and died very quick.

Father lay all day and night in a deep stupor, as if under the influence of some opiate, and could not be aroused to take any medicine. The Doctor said he could detect something on his breath that smelt very much like the contents of the vial that he had examined. How father could have gotten it was a mystery that could not be explained in any other way except that testified by the witch. The vial and contents was thrown into the fire, and instantly a blue blaze shot up the chimney like a flash of powder.

Father never revived or returned to consciousness for a single moment. He lingered along through the day and night, gradually wearing away, and on the morning of December 20th, 1820, breathed his last. Kate was around during the time, indulging in wild exultations and derisive songs. After father breathed his last nothing more was heard from Kate until after the burial was completed. It was a bright December day and a great crowd of people came to attend the funeral. Rev. Sugg Fort and Revs. James and Thomas Gunn conducted the services.

After the grave was filled, and the friends turned to leave the sad scene, the witch broke out in a loud voice singing, "Row me up some brandy O," and continued singing this until the family and friends had all entered the house. And thus ended one chapter in the series of exciting and frightful events that kept the whole neighborhood so long in a frenzy, and worked upon our fears from day to day.

## Kate's Departure and Return After Seven Years

After the death of John Bell, Sr., the fury of the witch was greatly abated. There were but two purposes, seemingly, developed in the visitation. One was the persecution of father to the end of his life. The other the vile purpose of destroying the anticipated happiness that thrilled the heart of Betsy. This latter purpose, however, was not so openly manifested as the first, and was of such a delicate nature that it was kept a secret as much as possible in the family and ignored when talked about. But it never ceased its tormenting until her young dream was destroyed. The witch remained with us after father's death, through the Winter and Spring of 1821, all the while diminishing or becoming less demonstrative. Finally it took leave of the family, bidding mother, "Luce," an affectionate farewell, saying that it would be absent seven years, but would surely return to see us and would then visit every house in the neighborhood. This promise was fulfilled as regards the old homestead, but I do not know that it visited other homes ill the vicinity.

It returned during February, 1828. The family was then nearly broken up. Mother, Joel and myself were the only occupants left at the old homestead, the other members of the family having settled off to themselves. The demonstrations announcing its return were precisely the same that characterized its first appearance. Joel occupied a bed in mother's room, and I slept in another apartment alone. After considerable scratching on the weatherboarding on the outside, it appeared in the same way on the inside, scratching on the bed post and pulling the cover from my bed as fast as I could replace it, keeping me up nearly all night. It went on in this way for several nights, and I spoke not a word about it, lest I should frighten mother. However, one night later, after worrying me for some time, I heard a noise in mother's room, and knew at once what was to pay.

Very soon mother and Joel came rushing into my room, much frightened, telling me about the disturbance and something pulling the cover off. We sat up till a late hour discussing the matter, satisfied that it was the same old Kate, and agreed not to talk to the witch, and that we would keep the matter a profound secret to ourselves, worrying with it the best we could, hoping that it would soon leave, as it did, after disturbing us in this way for some two weeks. This was my last experience with Kate. The witch came and went, hundreds of people witnessed its wonderful demonstrations, and many of the best people of Robertson and adjoining counties have testified to these facts, telling the story over and over to the younger generation, and for this and other reasons as before stated I have written this much of the details as correctly as it is possible to state the exciting events. So far no one has ever given any intelligent or comprehensive explanation of the great mystery. Those who came as experts were worse confounded than all others. As I before stated, a few mendacious calumniators were mean enough to charge that it was tricks and inventions of the Bell family to make money, and I write for the purpose of branding this version as an infamous falsehood. It was well known in the vicinity and all over the county that every investigation confirmed the fact that the Bell family were the greatest, if not the only sufferers from the visitation, and that no one, or a dozen persons in collusion, could have so long, regularly and persistently practiced such a fraud without detection, nor could they have known the minds and secrets of strangers visiting the place, and detailed events that were then occurring or had just transpired in different localities. Moreover the visitation entailed great sacrifice. As to how long this palavering phenomenon continued in the vicinity, I am unable to state. It did not disturb the remaining members of the family at the old place anymore. Mother died shortly after this and the house was entirely deserted, the land and other property being divided among the heirs. The old house stood for some years and was used for storing grain and other farm products, and was finally torn down and moved away. Many persons professed to have seen sights and heard strange sounds about the old house and in the vicinity all along up to this day. Several have described to me flitting lights along the old lane and through the farm, while others profess to have heard sounds of wonderfully sweet music and strange voices uttering indistinct word. And it is said that such things have been seen and heard at various places in the neighborhood, but I have no personal knowledge of the facts.

—RICHARD WILLIAMS BELL

# Chapter 9

*After John Bell's Death — The Lovers' Easter Monday — Prof. Powell's School — Uncle Zeke's Rectification of the Ghosts Disturbing the Fish — Several Weddings*

The death of John Bell, Sr., left a shadow of impenetrable gloom hanging like the pall of darkness over the sorrow stricken family. They were as a ship without a rudder; no solace for anguish and no light penetrating the darkness of the future, or forecasting the end of this great family affliction, save that the witch was now less viru lent in its demonstrations, ceasing to torment Betsy as it had before. The only way open was in pursuing the even tenor of life, awaiting the further developments of the unknown destroyer of the peace of the happy household. The death of Mr. Bell and the manner of his taking off awakened another sensation, one of a more serious and solemn import than all the events in the varied chapter of sensations that had so long kept the community in a state of frenzy, calling into exercise every faculty and all the stratagems of inventive genius, in the effort to detect the mysterious agency, only to be toiled and involved in still greater confusion. The phenomena had progressed, developing new features, power and character from week to week, finally fulfilling that malignant purpose declared in the outset to be a part of its mission, that of tormenting "Old Jack Bell" out of his life by a slow process of mysterious torture, and now all eyes and thoughts centered on Betsy, curiously wondering and dis cussing with animation the probable effect of the death of the father upon the daughter, and the attitude of the witch towards her. The girl was then overwhelmed with grief for the loss of a devoted father, which in the course of time was to be overcome, but the forebodings of the horrible witch, whose caprice might chasten her through life, or burst at any moment in the malignity of volcanic wrath, hung over her like an impending calamity, menacing the happiness, of life with bitter anguish. The suspense was dreadful in the extreme, like a horrifying nightmare haunting a feverish dream, and was not to be contemplated without a shudder. However, days and weeks passed, and neighbors continued their good offices, visiting and ministering comfort to the distressed family, and much to the surprise and gratification of all, there appeared a remarkable change in the mordacity of Kate toward Betsy. The haunting sphinx ceased harassing and become a ministering spirit, manifesting more sympathy, and tender compassion than all the friends who sought her on that gracious mission, save perhaps one. Joshua Gardner was never remiss in his devotions, and he labored with all the earnestness of his soul to remove the cloud that shadowed her happiness, and his efforts were not without good effect, notwithstanding his pres ence was attended with the premonition of Kate's abhorrent augury. Betsy Bell was conscious that her heart, beat in unison of sympathy for that manly devotion so freely bestowed on her. But what would be the consequence if she should disregard the warnings of her wicked tormentor, whose inflictions were already as great as could be endured? Might not the terrible freak execute its threats on her, as it had fulfilled the prophecy concerning her father, and destroy the peace and happiness of both herself and lover, rendering them miserable for life, should she yield to his entreaty and become his wife? Such were her thoughts and reasoning against the inclination of her cherished desire, and it was a most difficult problem to solve, in the struggle of the heart between love and fear. Kate had ceased meddling in the affair, never called Joshua's name to Betsy, nor spoke when he was present.

This relenting was encouraging to the lovers, and Joshua took advantage of the circumstance as evidence that the trouble was nearing the end, and pressed his suit, urging that the marriage should take place at an early date, when they might leave the haunted vale for their contemplated Western home, entering connubial life amid happier scenes full of new inspiration, and hearts thrilled with the joys they had So long anticipated. Betsy was disposed to yield to his persuasive reasoning; Joshua had drawn a different picture of the future from that which she had been looking upon. It was full of promise and stimulated renewed hope, and she gave her consent, conditionally, insisting that the matter be postponed a while longer, awaiting further developments in the witch's course, which were to be expected soon. There was, however, no more malevolent manifestations. Kate had almost ceased annoying the family, which served to give coloring to the rainbow of promise that Joshua painted so beautifully, and Betsy soon found her crushed hope reviving, animating her broken spirit. The flush returned to her paled cheeks, a brighter lustre filled her pretty blue eyes, while a mischievous smile returned to play in the light of those matchless orbs.

This change in Betsy was noticed by all comers and goers, and was the gossip of the neighborhood. The Fairy Queen of the

Haunted Dale was herself again. The gloom of despond had passed away, and a happy heart revealed itself in her sparkling eyes and merry laughter, which seemed to defy Kate, and the witch had ceased to interpose any further impediment to the match, and the brilliant wedding long anticipated was conceded to be close at hand. The Bell home had resumed something of its former gayety and splendid hospitality, extending a hearty welcome to all who came, offering the greatest attraction to visitors known in the country, and Betsy's grace of manners, pleasing conversation and charming wit, combined with her personal beauty, was a source of pleasure that all, old and young, delighted in.

> *She was the joy of the home,*
> *The pride of the vale;*
> *Her presence like sunshine*
> *That lights up the dale.*

## *Easter Monday*

Easter came in all the glory of ethereal April. Nature had put on its spring garb unusually early, and the day was like the resurrection morn, lending inspiration and vigor to all that was flush with life. The afternoon found a gay party of young people assembled at the Bell home, as by intuition, to arrange plans for the outing and pastime for the tomorrow, Easter Monday being a holiday observed by all people, even the servants being exempted from regular duty and allowed freedom to spend the day as they wished. A fishing excursion and a hunt for Wild flowers along the river bluff seemed to promise the greatest diversion, and it was agreed upon to meet at Brown's for the sport. The day dawned with a clear sky, and the sun rose in all of her splendor, sending forth gentle rays to kiss away the morning dew. The full blown orchard that almost surrounded the Bell residence presented a living bouquet of nature's beauty, white and pink blooms nestling amid the fresh young foliage of the trees, mingling their sweet perfumes on the gentle current that swept over the valley. Three interesting couples left the Bell place that morning for a stroll through the orchard and across the meadow to the river side, where the fishing party was expected to meet. The three couples were Betsy Bell and her lover, Joshua Gardner, Theny Thorn and Alex Gooch, and Rebecca Porter and James Long. Three happier couples never started out for a glorious holiday. Betsy had acceded to Joshua's proposition, dismissing all gloomy forebodings, and that morning for the first time wore a beautiful engagement ring, which Joshua placed on her finger Easter morning, while sitting beneath the favorite pear tree, and she started out with a light and joyous heart, full of mirthful sport, making merry the day.

"See there girls," exclaimed Betsy, "those beautiful pear trees, arrayed in white, representing the bride of the morning. They bow to us a hearty welcome this lovely holiday."

"Yes, I see," returned Theny Thorn, "they are perfectly lovely; but you overlook the peach trees on the other side of the path, dressed in pink. They represent the bridesmaids."

"Well," observed Becky Porter, "I should like to know what these pretty little violets represent which you all are unconsciously mashing under your big feet?"

"They are Cupid's arrows," answered Joshua Gardner. "They can not be crushed by trampling, Miss Becky; see how quick they rise up, smiling sweetly."

"Yes," exclaimed Betsy, "that is why I love them so much; break or bruise one, and it comes again as fresh as ever;"

Alex Gooch presumed that these sentimental expressions were inspired by the in vigorating morning breeze.

"Please, Miss Betsy, what does this refreshing zephyr, which blows such a pleasant gale, represent in your beautiful Easter picture?"

"Oh, that is the breath of the bridegroom," laughingly answered Betsy."

"Then," observed James Long, "if we are to judge from the fragrance of his breath, the bridegroom must be a distiller, out gathering nectar from the myriads of sweet blossoms, that excites so much felicitous exultation."

"Yes, Mr. Long," replied Becky, "you have a correct appreciation of the work of nature's God; you observe that the sun beams come first, gathering dewdrops from the precious buds, giving off the perfume to the morning's breath; that is what Betsy refers to."

"Oh, pshaw," ejaculated Alex Gooch, "please all hold up a bit and find your equilibrium. We started out to go fishing, but you girls are about to turn to fairies and take wings on the morning air."

"Yes, yes," exclaimed Joshua, "lets go fishing; why linger here. Look yonder, see those majestic trees that line the river bank, lifting up their leafy boughs in solid phalanx like a bordering mountain range of evergreen, keeping sentry over this lovely valley. See how gracefully their waving tops beckon us on to catch the sweet strains of the warbling birds that are mingling their melody with the soft sighing winds and the murmuring waves that are surging by."

"Hold up, hold up two minutes, Joshua; catch your breath and take a fresh start," exclaimed. Alex Gooch. "Oh, no," interposed James Long, "let Josh gush. He is in ecstasy of mind this morning, which accounts for his poetical flights."

"Well, said Miss Theny, "I am not going to leave here without a bouquet of Cupid's arrows. Come Becky, let's you and I load up with violets and peach blossoms, while Josh and Betsy are taking down that pear tree." Thus run the conversation in sallies of pleasantry and flights of fancy, as the three joyous couples wended their way through the orchard and across the green meadow to the river side, where many happy souls had already gathered and were making the best of the bright morning, entering fully into the frolicsome sports of the day.

## Prof. Powell's School

Very soon Prof. Richard Powell put in an appearance, just out from Springfield on his first canvass for the Legislature. He had heard something about the fishing party, and could not resist the temptation to call by, and mingle a short while with the happy throng of youngsters who had grown up under his tutorage. His presence was the signal for a general rush to the circle that was gathering around the handsome teacher who, though a bachelor, maintained his youthful appearance, good humor and fascinating manners, extending hearty greetings and happy congratulations.

"How good it is to be here," exclaimed the Professor; "it carries me back to our joyous school days, when you were all happy rollicking children, and I was well — I was one of you."

"We are all children yet," answered Joshua Gardner, "and I move that we open school right here and now."

"Good," said Alex Gooch, "I am in for that."

"And we will have some fun turning out the teacher," remarked Jimmie Long.

"No you won't," returned Betsy, "we girls will take Mr. Powell's part and turn you boys in for the ducking. What say you girls? All in favor of that motion hold up your strong right hand."

"Both hands," exclaimed Theny, and all hands went up. "There now boys," observed the Professor, "I have the advantage this time, and will not go into the river today. Betsy you are just the same sweet good girl you always were, taking my part against the boys, and you too, Theny, Becky, Betsy Gunn, Nicie Gooch, Mary Gotham, Sarah Batts; yes, and you too, Mahalia, Susan, Nancy, every one of those dear little hands; you are all my pets and sweethearts, and I am going to stand by you girls, as long as I live. If you should happen to marry these bad boys, and they don't treat you right, any of you, just call on me, and I will help to turn him out and put his head under the spring spout."

"Ha, ha," laughed Drew Bell, "I am going to be a girl today and help the Professor; put Calvin Johnson and Frank Miles under the spout, they have no business in this crowd anyway; they ought to be looking after some old girls."

"And where ought you to be, Drew? I just came down here thinking I would bait my hook with you for a catfish."

"No, no, Mr. Miles," exclaimed Betsy Gunn, "we can't spare Mr. Drew; he digs our fish bait; look at his hands."

"Hold up hands, Drew," cried Calvin Johnson; "if you are going to be a girl, hold up them hands."

"I shan't," said Drew. "Oh yes, Drew," insisted the Professor, "you have elegant hands."

"You mean elephant hands, Mr. Powell," returned Frank Miles."

"No, grubbing hoes," said another. "Flatboat oars," put in Alex Gunn."

"Call them what you please," spoke Becky Porter, "Mr. Drew can dig more fish bait than all of you, and we can't get along without him on Easter Monday."

"Why Becky," whispered Mary, "I guess you can get J. Long just as well."

"Now Mary, that's a good pun; what a witty Bell you might be," retorted Becky. "Please, Professor, excuse brother Drew from holding up his hands, he hasn't washed them to-day," pleaded Betsy. "Drew you will be excused, now finish digging bait; go to the spring and wash your hands, and then come to books, and fetch your gun to keep bad boys like Frank Miles off."

Thus an hour passed in the exchange of pleasantry, witticisms, congratulations, repartee and general hilarity, recounting amusing events that occurred during school days, Mr. Powell declaring that it was the happiest hour he had spent since he had left the neighborhood, and he was very sorry that he could not spend the day in such pleasant company, but that he was obliged to leave, and wishing all much good luck in the catch of the day, he was off; not, however, without paying Betsy Bell some special compliments, telling her that she had grown up to be more beautiful and charming than he had ever dreamed of when he used to pet her so much. "Just as I always told your mother, Miss Betsy, that you were the brightest and smartest girl in school, when she declared I would spoil you; but I did not, did I?"

"I think not, Professor; I hope I don't act like a spoilt girl," returned Betsy. "No you do not, Josh will bear me out in that. And by the way, Josh is a fine fellow; I have heard that you and Josh were about to make a match, and I shall wish you much hap piness and prosperity. That boy never could help loving you, and I never did blame him, as you were my little pet also, and I have waited almost as patiently as did Jacob for Rachel, hoping that you and Josh might forget that young school day love, but I have been disappointed, and now my request is to be at the wed ding. I want to be present when you wed, my little pet. Good-bye, I wish you well."

"Professor, I shall let you know when that happens," answered Betsy. As soon as Mr. Powell left, the assembly broke up in couples, stringing out along the river bank wherever good places could be found to throw in their hooks.

The darkies in the country were all out early for the holiday, and had monopolized the river bank from Brown's ford up to Gorham's mill, and the young people respecting their rights too much to disturb their pleasure, sought places below the ford, the three couples from the Bell home being last to locate, Joshua and Betsy taking the last position, just opposite the enchanted spring where the treasure trove was said to be concealed, which was a fair open spot. Mr. Gardner soon baited the hooks and set the poles in the bank to await the coming of the fish, and he and Betsy seated themselves on a green sward back upon the hillside over looking the fishing tackle. The sky continued clear, and the sun approached noontide, spreading bright rays over the valley, while a brisk wind heavily freighted with sweetest fragrance swept over, keeping the fresh green foliage of the tall trees along the river side in constant commotion. The modest little brook from the enchanted spring rippled down the riverbank in sweet consonance with the murmuring waves that rolled steadily by. The merry laughter of the gay throng strung out along the brink was caught up by the breeze in chorus with the music of the happy wildwood songsters that fluttered, chirped and twittered in the boughs overhead. It was indeed a real Easter day — the goddess of Spring restoring to nature that refreshing and renewal of life which so beautifully commemorates the resurrection of the world's Savior. Even the finny tribe seemed mindful of the commemorative event and were on a holiday frolic, coming to the top, jumping and flouncing on the bosom of the crystal-like waves, and didn't care a fig for the daintiest bait thrown out by eager fishermen. "Keep less noise down there, you'll frighten the fish away," yelled a stentorian voice in a commanding tone. "You are making more noise, Mr. Miles, than all of us," exclaimed Betsy Gunn. "Yes, but I have got to roar to get you youngsters settled so I can catch fish. Now you and John Bell settle, down to the business you came here for, like Josh and Betsy, I came to catch fish," returned Mr. Miles. "So did we," observed John, "but we have no idea of scaring them to death."

"That is just what you are doing; see how they jump," replied William Porter; "Frank and I came here to catch some fish if you chaps will make less noise."

"Then you will have to jump in and run them down, Brother Billy," exclaimed Becky Porter.

Uncle Zeke's Rectification On Dem Ghosts

Uncle Zeke, a consequential old darkey, who was very proud of the honor of being special valet to Rev. Thomas Gunn, occupied a position just above, to the right of Frank Miles, inquiringly put the question: "Mars Frank, can I have the 'sumption to pose you a question?"

"Yes, Uncle Zeke, what is it?"

"Well sar, Ize bin wanting to know how dem fishes jumpin' up out der kin hear us talkin' when they ain't got no ears?"

"I don't know, Uncle Zeke, but suppose it is by instinct or jar from the vibration of sound on the air; what do you think about it?"

"Well sar, Mars Frank, I was just lowin' da cud see fru dat water better dan da cud hear; den sar I was lowin' too dat dar war sumpen wrong wid dem fishes out dar, cause sir, you never seed fishes jump up dat way on holiday fo dis."

"What do you think is the matter, Uncle Zeke?"

"Well sar, an Injun spirit is out dar 'mong dem fish, dat's what's der matter, an they ain't goin' to bite today."

"Do you mean the old witch, Uncle Zeke?"

"Dat's exactly what it is, sar."

"How do you know that it's an Indian spirit?"

"Well sar, dat is der ruction in der case. Do you know dat der Injuns fust had dis country and dis river, an dat's why they named it Red River, cause it belonged to the red men?"

"Yes, but there is another story about the naming of this river which beats that. The story is that Moses Renfroe, who brought the first white settlement to this river, himself and all of his people were slaughtered by the Indians. The savage brutes dragged the men, women and children to the river, scalped their heads and cut their throats, throwing their bodies in, causing the water to run red with blood, and the stream was after that called Red River. That is what I understand about it, Uncle Zeke, but go on with your story, about the spirit."

"Well sar, dat's all der same; cause I was goin' to say, the Injuns was here fust, and we white fokes drove 'em out, all but dem what was dead and couldn't go, an they's here yet in der spirit. Ize had dis conjection under consideration ever since I fust heard Mars Tom prayin fur der witch to abrogate, an it tain't heard him yet, dat's what. When Mars Tom Gunn prays against the spirits and hit don't abrogate, den it hain't got no connection with Heaven."

"I think you are about right on that," approvingly replied Mr. Miles. "Well sar, dat is der rectification of dcm ghostes in my mind. You neber heard tell of Injuns in hell then, did you, Mars Frank?"

"Never did, Uncle Zeke."

"Well den, you neber seed one in hell, did you?"

"No, Uncle Zeke, I have not," returned Miles.

"Needer did Mars Tom. Cause he don't pray for em; den where is they? Why sar, dem dead Injuns who lived here are here yet, cause dey ain't got nowbar to go, an dat's what's der matter. I said soon as I heard about Corban Hall diggin up dem Injun bones over dar in the bottom, dar was goin' to be trouble."

"Have you ever seen the spirit, Uncle Zeke?" enquired Miles/

"Dat spirit what you call der witch? Yes sar, ain't you seed dem lights that move over the bottom on dark nights like a ball of fire? Well, dat's what it is, an you better not go about der except when you got a hair ball wid fox fire in it. That's der only way you kin fight dem spirits; jest like Dean does. Cause der Injun is like a black cat, he's got fire' in his eyes, fire in his back, an der devil in hiz neck, an you better let him alone. I said soon as I seed de Professor cum down here dis morning, dat dar warn't goin' to be no fish caught here today, an now you sees how dem fishes are jumpin' up."

"Why, Uncle Zeke, what has the Professor got to do with it?" enquired Miles.

"I tells you, Mars Frank, Ize a nigger and ain't got no business talkin', but I knows some things dat won't do to tell. Can't you see der spiritations in dat man's eyes? He didn't cum here for nuttin'. I hain't bin round here all dis time when der Professor kept school but know something, cause I've turned my witch ball on der phenomiter of dem ghostes, and seed dat man sperimentin' in der ruction of der spirits by der precunious instinction of der fungus, an every time he hit de Injun flint with the back of hiz knife he kotch der fire in hiz eyes; den when he looks on dat witch gal his eyes blazes, and den melts an dat put er spell on her."

Frank Miles laughed heartily at the idea, and told Uncle Zeke that his conclusions were no doubt correct.

During this interval, while time was swiftly passing, Joshua Gardner and Betsy Bell had not thought of their fishing tackle. They continued to occupy the velvety stratum first selected for a seat, oblivious to the merriment of their frolic some friends, and all the passing events that lent gayety to the occasion. Prof. Powell had observed that Betsy was wearing an engagement ring, and it was no doubt the sight of this token of a betrothal that inspired his remarks on taking leave of his "pet" that morning; and this was the subject that absorbed the thoughts of the lovers. They were discussing the wedding day, the far away home in the West that should soon give them welcome; the new scene that the change would bring, and the joys that awaited to bless their union. They were given entirely to the revelry of their own sweet dreams, bestowing no attention upon the surrounding charms. They took no notice of the finny tribe that played upon the rolling waves in sight, nor to the rippling of the wandering brook that gushed wildly down the hill from the foaming fountain above. Nor were they attracted by the warbling strains of the birds in the rustling boughs overhead, or interested in any of those things that afforded so much pleasure to other members of the company. They longed for the holly, for love's own sweet home in the faraway West, where they had:

> For Cupid built a flowery castle,
> Stored with manna of pure love,
> And strung Aeolian harps to sing
> Songs of the turtle dove.

## The Phantom Fish

Presently the sound of a mighty splashing was heard upon the waters that attracted all attention. A great fish had seized Joshua Gardner's hook with such force that it jerked the pole from the bank, and dashed off up stream, slashing the waves furiously as it rose to the top, flouncing and fluttering with great rage, and then diving to the bottom, carrying the pole under also, and instantly rising with a spurt, rushing in wild confusion to the south bank, as if it meant to leap for the and, but just at the water's edge it darted under, bounding up stream with the pole trolling behind, between the bank and the hooks thrown out by the eager fishermen along the stream. Passing under Uncle Zeke's tackle, the big swimmer flounced again to the top, making a hurry-scurry circle, tangling the old darkies' lines with the pole, and taking another straight shoot up the river. Before Uncle Zeke could recover from the confusion, one of his poles had joined in the procession, and he was bewildered with excitement. "Why don't you jump in, Uncle Zeke, and catch that fish and save your pole? Don't you see the fish is hung, and you are a good swimmer? Go quick, jump, plunge, and bring in the biggest fish ever caught in Red River," wildly shouted Frank Miles. This speech fired Uncle Zeke's courage to the highest pitch. He lost his head, and forgot all about the "Injun spirit" for the moment, and in less than a half minute had pulled off his coat and shoes and was in the act of jumping head-foremost into the river. But a precaution struck him, and he called a halt, carefully stepping one foot in the water, which he quickly jerked back with a shudder, and exclaiming, "I ain't goin' in der; I've done had a sentment 'bout dat fish, cepen its goin' to fool me."

"Oh go ahead, Uncle Zeke, don't be so cowardly; you belong to Parson Gunn, and what's the difference if you should drown, you will go straight to heaven," urged Mr. Miles.

"Dat's so, Mars Frank, I ain't carin' nuffin' 'bout drownin, but den whose goin' to tend to Mars Tom's hoss like I does, and who's goin' to brush his coat an' hat an' black high shoes? 'Cause their ain't nary another darkey that knows how to mix der lampblack; dat's what pesters me by der 'sentment." In the meanwhile a more youthful and daring darkey, a little higher up, heard Mr. Miles' suggestion and plunged in, swimming to the poles that were still bobbing up and down in the water, and as he grabbed the main pole, the fish made a circle, tightening the line, and whirling the Negro around in the water, as it made another dash for the bank, helping the darkey to swim with greater ease and speed. But just as he reached the shore, and the excited crowd had gathered to help land the catch, the great fish flounced to the top, releasing itself, and was gone dashing up stream, splitting the waves, amid the shouts of excited fishermen nearly up to Gorham's mill. Now an excited discussion turned upon the antics of the monster aquatic, its size, and to which family of the finny tribe it belonged. One thought it was an "eel," another said "catfish," another said a shark had wandered up the stream.

Frank Miles declared that it was the biggest trout ever seen, but all agreed that the great finny was between two and three feet in length. William Porter observed that they had all better get to their places and bait their hooks; that the fish might return soon. The suggestion was sufficient, and pretty soon quiet was restored, everyone giving strict attention to fishing. But Uncle Zeke could not suppress the inclination to whisper to Frank Miles, "I tole you so. I said sumptin' war goin' to happen."

Joshua and Betsy had been attracted from their delightful repose by the prevailing excitement, but as soon as the big finny made its escape, they returned to the beautiful sward, ostensibly to look after the remaining fishing tackle. Betsy, however, did not seem so gay and happy as she had appeared all the morning, and frankly confessed to her lover strange forebodings that depressed her feelings, but she could not explain the cause. Joshua then devoted his efforts to dispelling the gloom, as he had before done, and at the moment he had quite well succeeded, when the reverberating sound of ecstatic voices above were heard in wild exclaim, "Look out, look out, its coming back!" The breaking waves and the furious lashing of the water told the story, that the playful fish was on its return down stream, riding upon the tide, as if to catch the sunbeams that glittered upon the foamy crest. It, however, quickly disappeared, and all was quiet, every fisherman anxiously watching for a bite.

## The Lovers' Forebodings

The dying excitement of the last appearance left the lovers in a reverie of their own thoughts, deeply meditating upon their contemplated plans, as if trying to penetrate a shadow that seemed to hang heavily over their destiny, in spite of all efforts to rise above the crest of the cloud by looking all the while at the bright side. The suspense was painful, but nothing to compare with the sound of Kate's familiar voice which immediately pierced their ears like the bursting of a thunder cloud, pleading in that same old plaintive tone, "Please Betsy Bell, don't have Joshua Gardner," repeating the entreaty over and over, until the lovers were overwhelmed with dismay, when the melancholy voice died away gradually as the waves rolled by and were lost to sight with the passing current. The color faded from the poor girl's checks as quickly as if a dagger had pierced her bosom, and Joshua, though courageous as he had proven before on similar occasions, felt the pangs of a broken heart, and was powerless to sooth the anguish that told so plainly on his affianced.

They sat motionless and speechless for some minutes, as if awaiting an awful doom. At last Betsy broke the silence, proposing a walk up the hillside to the spring for a drink of water. There they drank and discoursed on the excellence of the cooling draught, the beauty of the foaming bubbles that broke away in diminutive billows rushing with the trickling stream down the craggy hillside, then gathering a few wild flowers, and thus they whiled away some twenty minutes in an effort to dispel the gloomy fore bodings and regain composure, but all was in vain. Finally Betsy summoned the courage of her convictions, telling Joshua frankly that her mind was made up, and that she could not brook the storm which threatened all the fancied happiness which seemed to be in store for them; that she was now clearly convinced that her tormenter would follow her through life with an appalling destiny, should she resist its importunities and dire threatenings, just as it had already afflicted her, and brought her father to suffering and unto death. Even were she able to endure it all, her compliance with his wish would be an injustice to Joshua, and a wrong for which she could never expect forgiveness. Therefore she desired to with draw her promise and return to him the engagement ring that she prized so highly. Joshua Gardner was suffering the bitterest anguish that ever pierced a heart. He had never known before the strength of his passion for the queenly beauty who stood before him in the perfection of lovely young womanhood, conscious that the stern decision had cost her as much pain as it did him, and was rendered as a sacrifice for his own welfare, as she conceived. He tried to plead his cause anew, but was so overwhelmed with the force of her reasoning and firmness of decision that he for the first time faltered, realizing that all hope was vain, and that every plea but added another sorrow to a bleeding heart, and a fresh pang to his own, and he gracefully accepted the inevitable, begging her to keep the ring in memory of one who loved her dearer than his own life. This she declined to do, telling him that the ring was a seal to her solemn vow, and the vow could not be broken in the sight of heaven, unless he would accept the return of the ring. "I could not," she said, "retain it without retaining the thorn that now pierces my heart and I know Joshua that you are too generous not to accede to my wish." Slipping it from her finger as she held out her hand, Joshua Gardner in all the bitter anguish of a broken heart, exclaimed, "Betsy, my love, the adoration of my soul, the long hope of my life, this is the bitterest draught of all, but for your sake I drink to the dregs, releasing you from the promise which I know was earnest." Thus ended the affair in which the witch had manifested so much interest from the commencement of the "Family Trouble."

Very soon the three couples retraced their steps across the valley to the Bell home, amid the gay scenes of nature in the full flush of joyous Spring, but the walk was not attended by that levity and buoyancy of spirit which characterized the morning stroll. All were conscious of the shadow which hung so heavily over Betsy, depressing her happy spirit, and which had that day sent another poisonous shaft quivering to her bleeding heart, and the bowed form and dejected spirit of Joshua Gardner, which told plainly that he too carried a crushed heart in his manly bosom, and all hearts were touched too deep with burning sympathy to admit of any alacrity. It was more like going to a funeral, and the accompanying couples kept a respectful distance in the rear, discussing as they walked leisurely along the appalling sorrow which the return of the witch had brought that day. The lovers separated that afternoon never to meet again. A few days later, as soon as he could arrange his affairs, Joshua Gardner took his departure, several days journey to the west, and settled in West Tennessee, the place now known as Gardner's Station, Obion county, where he passed a long and honorable career, esteemed by the people for his true manhood and moral worth. He died several years ago at the advanced age of eighty-four years.

> The weird fiend, cast the scene,
> Lurid with the seer's blight.
> And hope forlorn, shadowed the morn
> With the gloom of night.
> Thus the sequel, young love unequal
> To the wizard's subtle art.
> And dreamers await, the hand of fate,
> While despondency sears the heart.
>
> The lovers parted, weary, broken-hearted,
> Cruel fate coming between.
> The blasting frost, the appalling ghost,
> Chilled the bower of green.
> The flowers withered, the castle quivered
> When Cupid fled the scene.
> And the beautiful tower, lovers bower
> Became a fading, crumbling sheen.
>
> Seizing the wreck, scuttling the deck
> Witches vaunted ghoulish spleen.
> The vile freak, with exulting shriek
> Cavorted the dale unseen.
> The jack-o-lantern glare, flitted the air.
> O'er the valley of doom.
> And the pall of night, shadowed beacon light
> Filling the vale with gloom.

*Down the hill and o'er the rill*
*    Horrid spirits delighted to prowl,*
*The piercing thrill, of whippoorwill,*
*    Giving place to the hooting owl.*
*From the mill and old still*
*    Came songs of the weird,*
*Voices shrill, with horrible trill*
*    Hushing the joyous mocking bird.*

*The old pear tree, hoary it be,*
*    Still shadows the happy scene,*
*Spreading its boughs, over the vows*
*    Witnessed beneath its green.*
*Where lovers plighted, hearts united,*
*    The vows they would redeem.*
*And continues weeping, lovers sleeping,*
*    For the return of the dream.*

The witch exulted freely over the victory won, but troubled Betsy no more; rather tried to soothe and strengthen her depressed spirit, promising to leave soon, as it did, bidding the family goodbye.

## *Several Weddings*

Some months later a brilliant wedding took place at the residence of James Johnson. The whole community gathered in to celebrate the nuptials that united Theny Thorn and Alex Gooch. Six months after this affair, James Long and Rebecca Porter were happily wedded. Both couples settled in the Bell neighborhood, sharing the burdens of good citizenship, and their descendants still reside in that community, worthily sustaining the honored names inherited, ranking among the best people of the county. Next followed the marriage of John Bell, Jr., and Elizabeth Gunn, whose honorable career and success in life is recorded in the family biography.

It was a long while before Betsy Bell could overcome the shock of that notable Easter Monday in April 1821, which almost extinguished that effervescence which had characterized her girlhood. Vivacious as she was, it was difficult for her to conceal the depression that had so long menaced her young life and overwhelmed her on that memorial day. Some while after this, however, the Professor, Hon. Richard Powell, became her persistent suitor and was finally accepted, and in this she kept her promise that the Professor should be at the wedding. Richard Powell was many years her senior, but was a handsome gentleman of elegant manners, and bore all honorable name and reputation. He was in fact a leading character and politician, represented the county several times, or as long as he desired, in the State Legislature, which was then considered a very high honor. He was also prominent in all public affairs, and one of the most popular men in Robertson County. Their married life was comparatively short, about seventeen years. Mr. Powell died, and Betsy remained a widow the balance of her life. About 1875 she moved to Mississippi, where one of her children and other relatives resided, and died in 1890 at the age of eighty-six years. She has grandchildren still living in Robertson county, who have inherited that vivacity and charming wit which characterized her young life. After mature years, Mrs. Powell became a large fleshy woman, and physically very stout. She was high spirited and noted through life for her industrious habits, good nature, and splendid social qualities, always entertaining in any circle. The fearful thing known as "The Family Trouble," so called to this day by the descendants, was the plague of her life. She had borne with great fortitude and womanly courage the afflictions visited upon her, but the story set afloat by parties failing in their investigations, charging her with the authorship of the mystery, after she had submitted to all manner of tests, was crushing to her strong spirit, yet she murmured not, hoping to live down the misrepresentation, and that her innocence would be demonstrated to all intelligent reasonable people, and so it was to the people of Robertson County, acquainted with the facts, but a mischievous lie once set afloat travels far beyond the reach of truth. So it was in her case; wherever the story of the witch had gone among strangers, her name has been coupled with it as the author of those most wonderful demonstrations, and all through her long life the story was frequently revived, which to her was like a canker worm that never ceased torturing; and still she endured it patiently. However, the time came when patience ceased to be a virtue.

About 1849 the Saturday Evening Post, published either at Philadelphia or New York, printed a long sketch of the Bell Witch phenomenon, written by a reporter who made a strenuous effort in the details to connect her with the authorship of the demonstrations. Mrs. Powell was so outraged by the publication that she engaged a lawyer to institute suit for libel. The matter, however, was settled without litigation, the paper retracting the charges, explaining how this version of the story had gained credence, and the fact that at the time the demonstrations commenced Betsy Bell had scarcely advanced from the stage of childhood and was too young to have been capable of originating and practicing so great a deception. The fact also that after this report had gained circulation, she had submitted to any and every test that the wits of detectives could invent to prove the theory, and all the stratagems employed, served only to demonstrate her innocence and utter ignorance of the agency of the so-called witchery, and was herself the greatest sufferer from the affliction.

# Chapter 10

## *Negro Stories: The Experiences of Uncle Dean, the Rail Splitter*

Rev. James Byrns, in his graphic sketch, intimates that the Negroes gave the most thrilling accounts of the witch operations, but he seems to regard Negro testimony as unreliable and declines to quote their sayings; on general principles no doubt. But in this the good man is mistaken. He has not studied the Negro character along this line. The colored brother may prevaricate in regard to a chicken roost; he may be extravagant in describing a coon fight; he may dilate humorously on his possum dog; he may spin fine yarns about the golden pavements in the New Jerusalem and the angels sopping possum gravy with ash cakes and "taters;" he may mislead one in regard to the contents of his gourd bottle; he may be weak on the subject of watermelons, and tell fine stories on Bre'r Rabbit sitting in the fence corner picking briars out of his feet, but when it comes to haunts, he is the most reliable witness on earth. The Negro may be off and crooked on some things, but under no circumstance will he tell a lie on a ghost, nor deviate a single hair's breadth from the truth in establishing the existence of the spooks. The purpose of the writer is to go to the bottom of this witch history and give all of the inside facts, and this cannot be done if Sambo is ignored. No such a history would be complete without the stories of Uncle Dean, the famous rail-splitter, and trusty servant of John Bell, who had many contacts with the witch. Therefore the writer paid a special visit to Aunt Ibby Gunn, who was a servant of Alex Gunn, and resides at Cedar Hill, Tenn., with her children, happy and cheerful, and at this writing is eighty-six years of age, as appears from the Gunn family record — born October 25, 1806. She was the younger sister of Dean's wife, Kate. They were daughters of Uncle Zeke, a pompous old darkie who belonged to Rev. Thomas Gunn, and felt elevated by the pious and dignified character of his master.

## *Dean and the Black Dog Witch*

Aunt Ibby is the only survivor of the Negro families who lived in that vicinity in the beginning of the Witch history. Being approached on the subject she replied: "'Course I members 'bout dar witch, cause it cum wid Dean to see hiz wife, fur she was my sister, an' I done want no mo' boderation by dem spirits nudder, I don't."

Aunt Ibby was disposed to stop at this. She did not care to discuss haunts, lest the demons might return to disturb her. Being assured, however, that the witch had become very rich and aristocratic, and had long since gone to Europe on a pleasure trip, promising not to return during her lifetime, she consented to tell some things that Dean said about it.

"De fust time Dean seed der speritation, he sed it appeared like a big black dog, jest trottin' 'long afore him tipity tipity tip, to de door, an' den banish. Dean sed how he warn't 'fraid, but I seed he ware mighty pale; den he tuck to fetchin' hiz axe, kase dat dog cum wid him eber time, an' den banish, sorter pericatin' in der transfiction, jest gwine all ter pieces, risin' like sparks when yer chunk der fire. Den hit got to pesterin' old Mister Bell so bad, jabbin' all der vitals outen hiz mouf wid a stick, Dean was sorter confuscated 'bout what ter do, cause dat sort uv carrication wuz pecteratin' on der appetude, an' spoilin' er heap of good eatin'. Den Kate, she tuck and made Dean a witch ball outen her hair, an' put in sum spunk, foxfire and such, and some brimstone an' camfire, den wrapped hit all ober wid yarn an' hair, an' gave Dean der ball tu keep der dog frum hurtin' him. So der nex night, cumin' long der road whistlin' he wuz, sumpen said, 'Dean, what makes you whistle so lonesum, jest dar away.' Dean sez, 'Kase ize gwinter see my wife.' Den hit sez, 'Dean what's dat yous got in yer pocket?' Dean sez, 'Nullin'.' Den hit sez, 'Dean you knows dat's er lie, kase yous got foxfire wrapped up in yer wife's hair tu pester me. I'll sho you Mr. Smarty you can't congergate me dat way,' jest so. Dean he got down on hiz knees tu pray. Den hit sez, 'Lord Jesus, Dean, what er fool yer is; done yer know yer can't pray like ole Sugar Mouf? Git up frum dar an' sho yer foxfire.' Sez Dean, sez he, just so 'In der name of der Lord what's yer gwine ter do tu me?' Den it sez, 'Cepen you give me dar ball, Ise gwine ter turn you tu a hoss an' ride you cross der river to der stillhouse.' Den Dean tuck der ball outen hiz pocket, an' hit commenced swellin' bigger 'an er fodder stack, an' he had ter drap it, he did, an' der ball busted an' tuck fire, blazin' up, an' almost stunk hiz bref away, But dat warnt nuffin'; dar wuz dar same black dog wid his mouf wide open grinnin' jest redy tu jump on 'im, an' Dean, he cum down wid hiz axe, he did, and split dar dog's head wide open, an' staved der axe clear down in der ground so deep he coulden' find it no more. De dog, he turned ober an' ober three times, kicked, an' den jumped up 'mose outer sight an' fell kerflop on dat foxfire, an' der ball riz right up an' shot off in er blaze like er star. Dean, he lit out, he did, and he never stopped till he run agin der door an' busted hit wide open, an' fell on der floor, pale as er white sheet. For God! Dat nigger's eyes done come clean outen hiz head. Kate, she tuck to rubbin' him wid camfire an' old berdildoc 'til he cum to his self an' told all about this, an' der next time Dean seed dat dog, it had two heads."

## How Dean Was Turned into a Mule

Dean had another thrilling and most frightful experience with the witches, which he told to Alex Gunn and others, after relating the same transaction described in Aunt Ibby's interview. Said he, "I told Kate an' Uncle Zeke 'bout how dat ball tuck fire shootin' off wid dat dog after I split his head open, an' sartin az your bawned, Mars Alex, but fur dat ball I'd been a gone nigger. Den Kate she tuck an' made me a nudder ball an' put some other spiritifications in it, 'cept them what wus in der first ball; some sort er Injun congerations jest like her fader said. Den she told me dat der witch couldn't do nuffin long as I kept dat ball in my pocket; an' if I give it up any mo dar wud be der last of me, jest so. Den I tuck der ball in my pocket, I did, feelin' pretty certain it was gwinter stay der dis time, an' it did. Den sar, Mars Alex, der nex time I went by der wood pile an' tuck my axe on my shoulder, cause I depends a heap on my axe, an' went along outen der gate whistlin like I didn't care fur nuffin, an' goin' along up der lane, dar sat dat same black dog wid two heads an' both moufs open grinnin at me, he wuz, showin' his big white teeth. I sorter stopped, I did, Den sez I, 'In der name of der Lord what's dat?' Jest so, den sumpen sed, 'Dean you can't pass here cepten you give me dat ball in yo pocket,' Jest so, den I 'membered what Kate an' Uncle Zeke said how der witch couldn't do nuffin cepen hit got my ball. Sez I, 'What's yo name?' 'My name is Black Dog; you knows me, you black rascal, cause you's done an' split my head open wid yo axe,' Jest so, den sez I, 'I haut got no ball, yo tuck it tudder time.' Den it sez, 'You's a liar Dean, I knows you's done an' got er hudder ball worsser dan der fust one, cause you is dun an' fetched er whole heap of trouble on me.' Den sez I, 'If you won't lemme pass, I kin go back.' Jest so, den I sorter walked backwards, back, back, back, tel I got clean outen sight, an' den turned round ter run. An' befo' God dar was dar same dog on tudder side wid his mouth wide open. I tells you, Mars Alex, I felt a heep wusser, like I wus kerflumuxed, but it warnt goin' to give up, an' I jest resolved in my mind to fight it out, cause dar warnt no udder choice. Den sez I, 'What you want?' Jest so, den it sez, 'Cepen you gimme dar ball Ise gwinter turn you to a hoss an' ride you ober der river to der still-house.' Den I membered again what Kate an' Uncle Zeke said, how dar want no dependence in what a Injun spirit said, an' if I give up dat ball I'd be a dead nigger right dar, cause dat ghost ware mad. Den I solved to depend on dat ball and my axe, and sed, 'I ain't goin' ter give you my ball,' an' I'll split you clean open tu der tail cepen you git outen my way,' Jest so, den hit sez, 'Say yer prayers Dean, an' I commenced gittin' weak, an' draped my axe, cause I felt er curious spell creepin' on me. Den sumpen sed, 'Pick up your axe Dean,' and I stooped ober feelin fur der axe an' cudden find it, an' cudden git up no mo, an' dar I stood on my hands an' feet. Den sumpen sed, 'He's tu high behind to tote dubble.' Er hudder sed, 'Dat's all right, level im down.' Den sumpen jerked my tail, an' I kicked backwards wid one foot an' hit fell kerflop in der road. Bout dis time der ole jack brayed an' one witch sed, 'Dar, bad luck, dat spoilt der job; he's nuffin but er dam mule.' T'other one said, 'Well, you can't make nuffin but er mule outen er dam nigger, no how.' Den da commenced cussin' an' fussin' 'bout which one was gwinter ride befo an' behind. One says, 'Der mule hain't got no main fur sturips an' bridle ter hold to, an' my arms are too short to catch his ears.' Den da both hopped up; de little witch got on behind an' sed, 'Now les ride him to hell fur breakfast.' Den de big witch stretched both hands out an' tuck me by der ears, an' quicker dan da knowed nuffin, I tucked my head, jumped backwards, an' kicked them clean over my back, an' sat dem witches down ca-whallup on tudder side of der fence in der field, an' I tuck out and went tearin' up der lane, an' never stopped runnin' tell I got to Kate's door an' commenced pawin' till I pawed der door open, an' there sat Kate mendin' my old britches, an' seein' her by der light it tuck der spell off, and I was myself again. I tells you, Mars Alex, but fur Kate's hair ball dem witches would of rid me all night, an' where wud I be now? When I heard dem talkin 'bout ridin' me to hell fur breakfast I was der most scared mule you eber seed, cause it appeared like a mighty long rocky road down hill for me ter tote double an' skip in before sun up. Den I didn't know 'bout cumin back any mo. Den what wud I look like walkin' round dar among gentlemen wid my ole rail-splittin' clothes on? What would ole master say when he got up an' found me missin'? I tells you, Mars Alex, it ware a mighty solemn confusion what perigated round my 'prehension 'bout dat time."

## How Dean Got His Head Busted

There are many persons still living in Robertson County who re-member Uncle Dean. He lived to a very old age, and was noted throughout the surrounding country as the famous rail-splitter, a distinction which he was very proud of, though it did not elect him to the presidency of the United States. However, had he lived in later years, he might have walked Abraham Lincoln's log. The Negroes and children in the neighbor hood delighted in gathering around the old darkie to hear his hair-raising witch stories. Dean carried a prominent scar on his forehead, which gave his physiog-nomy a very conspicuous cast. A good lady connected with the Bell family, describing Dean to the writer, says he declared to the day of his death that this scar was caused by an unpleasant contact with "Kate," the witch, in which he was knocked in the head with a big stick. Dean was a great possum hunter; Autumn came in all of its glory. The luscious persimmon was ripe, and possums fat and plen-tiful, and Dean's heart panted for the woods, as did his appetite long for "possum and taters." His mind was bent on a round with the "varments," but a very serious dilemma was presented in the contemplation of the sport. His experience with "Black Dog" warned him of the danger in venturing out without his witch ball, and it was certain that no game could be found if he carried it; no dog could trail a possum after catching the scent of a witch ball. So it was, Dean turned the matter over and over in his mind, and kept a sharp lookout for "Kate." He determined to make use of the first favorable opportunity that presented. Finally the time came. Hear-ing the Witch in the house carrying on at a great rate with the visi-tors, he concluded that was the opportunity to make a short round, and return before "Kate" adjourned the meeting. So he swung his axe over his shoulder, whistled to old Caesar and struck out. Next morning Dean was missing, and Mr. Bell was very uneasy for a time, but soon after breakfast he showed up with a great gash in his cranium and was very bloody.

"What's the matter now Dean?" inquired Mr. Bell.

"De witch dun had me for a fact, ole mars, an for God's sake, it liked ter killed me, it did. 'Cepten fur thinken 'bout whose gwinter split der rails, I specs that I'd of given up. 'Cause I knowed dar warn't gwinter be no mo rails split here 'cepten I done it. Dat's all dat saved me sar, fur a fact it was."

"How did it happen Dean?" again inquired Mr. Bell.

"Well ole mars, Ise gwinter to tell der truf 'bout it, dar I iz. For

God sake, it was jest dis way. I heard de ole witch in der house speakin' wid de white folks 'bout religion. Den I concluded it was a mighty good time ter go out an kotch er possum fur dinner Sunday, supposin' I cud git back before de witch knowed it. So I slips off round der field, an' directly old Caesar he treed a big possum up on top of dat high stump side of der fence. I jest left him dar, cause I knowed he warn't gwinter git away from ole Caesar. Den I tuck an' cut down a little saplin' 'bout six foot long, an' split one end of it, den tuck der possum down an' pull his tail through der split, an layed him down ter git my axe. Den I hears sumpen' cummin' down other side of de fence, tipity tipity tip, tipity tipity tip, and der next ting I knowed, dar stood a great big ole rabbit, an' Caesar he tuck out he did. Den I knowed sumpen war gwinter happen, cause dar dog neber lef me fo dis. Den de old rabbit said, 'Hello, Kernel Possum, what's all er dat ornamentation you got on yer tail?' Jest so, den der possum said, "Oh Kernel Rabbit, Ise so glad yous cum; dis ain't no ornamentation, hit am er split stick Dean put on my tail to keep me from gittin away. Oh it am hurtin so bad. Please Kernel take hit off.' Den Kernel Rabbit, he said, 'Why ain't you like me, Kernel Possum; don't hab no tail, den de niggers cant put split stick on yer.' Den Kernel Possum sed, 'If I done hab no tail like you, how's I gwinter hold on to der limbs an shake 'simmons down fur you? 'Dat's so,' sez Kernel Rabbit, 'jest take er way.' Den Kernel Rabbit. he commenced swellin' like blowin' up like a bladder, tell he got bigger den Mars Frank Miles, an' he tuck holt of dat stick and jerked der split wide open, he did, an told Kernel Possum to go on an shake dat 'simmon tree. Den he turned round to me, Kernel Rabbit did, an sez, 'Dean, I'll learn you sum sense 'bout puttin' er poor possum's tail in der split stick. Next thing you'll be twisten' all of my hide off tu get me outen de hollow.' Den he hit me kerwhack on der head wid dat stick, an I knowed nuffin' mo 'til sun up."

This explanation satisfied "old mars," and he told Dean to go to Aunt Chloe and let her bandage his head, and lay up until he got well, and hereafter always wrap the possum's tail around his thumb and carry it in his hand, and never draw another one through the split of a stick. From that day to this, no one in this part of the country has been guilty of the barbarous act of drawing a "po" possum's tail through the split of a stick, or of twisting a rabbit out of a hole.

# Chapter 11

## Gen. Andrew Jackson: Remarkable and Amusing Incidents Attending the Great Soldier and Statesman's Visit to the Witch, and Other Reminiscences

Col. Thomas L. Yancey, a prominent lawyer of the Clarksville, Tenn., bar, who is closely related to the Fort family, was raised in the Bell settlement, and has been familiar with the stories of the witch as told by different witnesses from his youth up, contributes the following interesting sketch from notes taken with a view to writing the history. In addition to the visit of Gen. Jackson and party, it will be observed that he confirms the statements of three other parties in regard to Dr. Sugg's experience:

CLARKSVILLE, TENN.
JAN. 1, 1894
M. E INGRAM — DEAR SIR:
    In answer to your inquiry as to what I know about the Bell Witch excitement of many years ago, I will state that I was born within four miles of the John Bell home, where the witch is said to have disported itself to the terror of many good and pious souls. While quite a young man I became much interested in the stories my relatives and other people told in regard to the phenomenon, which I had heard repeated from my earliest recollection, and ambitious in my youth to discover the cause and write a history of the affair, I determined to enter into the investigation, and did some forty years ago undertake the matter, gathering many amusing and strange incidents, but not sufficiently connected and au thenticated to justify my purpose. I soon learned that Williams Bell was the only person who had kept a diary of what transpired, and had written the facts, leaving the manuscript with his wife or some member of his family at his death. Of course I was anxious to get the paper, and not being acquainted with Williams Bell's widow, I applied to Squire John Bell, Jr., to know if such manuscript was in existence, and if it could be had for publication. He informed me that his brother had written the facts, etc., regarding the mystery, and that Washington

Lowe, a lawyer of Springfield, had applied for it and been refused. He thought, however, he could induce his brother's family to let him have it, and promised to intercede for me. Some time after this he told me that he could not get it, that the family refused to let him or any one have it, and after this I gave up the purpose of writing a book and pursued the investigation no further. However, I remember some very graphic stories told by the old people who visited the scene often, stated as having absolutely occurred, and told in all seriousness by persons whose veracity I could not doubt. My grandfather, Whitmel Fort, told me that he visited the place often during the excitement, meeting with many persons from a distance who came to investigate the witch. Grandfather said he could in no way account for the phenomena. There was no doubt of the fact that some thing persecuted Miss Betsy Bell terribly after she retired to bed. He went with others to her relief amid her outcries of agony, and they all could not hold the bed covering on her, so powerful was the unseen object in pulling it off. Even could this have been accounted for, the keen ringing sound like that of a hand slapping her jaws when she would scream with pain, and the deep red splotches left on her cheeks, were mysterious beyond comprehension.

Grandfather Fort also told me the story of Gen. Jackson's visit to the witch, which was quite amusing to me. The crowds that gathered at Bell's, many coming a long distance, were so large that the house would not accommodate the company. Mr. Bell would not accept any pay for entertaining, and the imposition on the family, being a constant thing, was so apparent, that par ties were made up and went prepared for camping out. So Gen. Jackson's party came from Nashville with a wagon loaded with a tent, provisions, etc., bent on a good time and much fun investi gating the witch. The men were riding on horseback and were following along in the rear of the wagon as they approached near the place, discussing the matter and planning how they were going to do up the witch, if it made an exhibition of such pranks as they had heard of. Just then, within a short distance of the house, traveling over a smooth level piece of road, the wagon halted and stuck fast. The driver popped his whip, whooped and shouted to the team, and the horses pulled with all of their might, but could not move the wagon an inch. It was dead stuck as if welded to the earth. Gen. Jackson commanded all men to dismount and put their shoulders to the wheels and give the wagon a push.

The order was promptly obeyed. The driver laid on the lash and the horses and men did their best, making repeated efforts, but all in vain; it was no go. The wheels were then taken off, one at a time, and examined and found to be all right, revolving easily on the axles. Another trial was made to get away, the driver whipping up the team while the men pushed at the wheels, and still it was no go. All stood off looking at the wagon in serious meditation, for they were "stuck." Gen. Jackson after a few moments thought, realizing that they were in a fix, threw up his hands exclaiming, "By the eternal, boys, it is the witch." Then came the sound of a sharp metallic voice from the bushes, saying, "All right General, let the wagon move on, I will see you again tonight." The men in bewildered astonishment looked in every direction to see if they could discover from whence came the strange voice, but could find no explanation to the mystery. Gen. Jackson exclaimed again, "By the eternal, boys, this is worse than fighting the British." The horses then started unexpectedly of their own accord, and the wagon rolled along as light and smoothly as ever. Jackson's party was in no good frame of mind for camping out that night, notwithstanding one of the party was a professional "witch layer," and boasted much of his power over evil spirits, and was taken along purposely to deal with Kate, as they called the witch. The whole party went to the house for quarters and comfort, and Mr. Bell, recognizing the distinguished character of the leader of the party, was lavishing in courtesies and entertainment. But Gen. Jackson was out with the boys for fun and "witch hunting" was one of them for the time. They were expecting Kate to put in an appearance according to promise, and they chose to set in a room by the light of a tallow candle waiting for the witch. The witch layer had a big flintlock army or horse pistol, loaded with a silver bullet, which he held steady in hand, keeping a close lookout for Kate. He was a brawny man, with long hair, high cheekbones, hawk-bill nose and fiery eyes. He talked much, entertaining the company with details of his adventures, and exhibitions of un daunted courage and success in overcoming witches. He exhibited the tip of a black cat's tail, about two inches, telling how he shot the cat with a silver bullet while sitting on a bewitched woman's coffin, and by stroking that cat's tail on his nose it would flash a light on a witch the darkest night that ever come; the light, however, was not visible to any one but a magician. The party was highly entertained by the vain stories of this dolt. They flattered his vanity and encouraged his conceit, laughed at his stories, and called him sage, Apollo, oracle, wiseacre, etc. Yet there was an expectancy in the minds of all left from the wagon experience, which made the mage's stories go well, and all kept wide awake till a late hour, when they became weary and drowsy, and rather tired of hearing the warlock detail his exploits. Old Hickory was the first one to let off tension. He commenced yawning and twisting in his chair. Leaning over he whispered to the man nearest him, "Sam, I'll bet that fellow is an arrant coward. By the eternals, I do wish the thing would come, I want to see him run." The General did not have long to wait. Presently perfect quiet reigned, and then was heard a noise like dainty footsteps prancing over the floor, and quickly following, the same metallic voice heard in the bushes rang out from one corner of the room, exclaiming, "All right, General, I am on hand ready for business." And then addressing the witch layer, "Now, Mr. Smarty, here I am, shoot." The seer stroked his nose with the cat's tail, leveled his pistol, and pulled the trigger, but it failed to fire. "Try again," exclaimed the witch, which he did with the same result. "Now its my turn; lookout, you old coward, hypocrite, fraud. I'll teach you a lesson." The next thing a sound was heard like that of boxing with the open hand, whack, whack, and the Oracle tumbled over like lightning had struck him, but he quickly recovered his feet and went capering around the room like a fright ened steer, running over everyone in his way, yelling, "Oh my nose, my nose, the devil has got me. Oh Lordy! He's got me by the nose." Suddenly, as if by its own accord, the door flew open and the witch layer dashed out, and made a beeline for the lane at full speed, yelling every jump. Everybody rushed out under .the excitement, expecting the man would be killed, but as far as they could hear up the lane, he was still running and yelling, "Oh Lordy." Jackson, they say, dropped down on the ground and rolled over and over, laughing. "By the eternal, boys, I never saw so much fun in all my life. This beats fighting the British." Presently the witch was on hand and joined in the laugh. "Lord Jesus," it exclaimed, "How the old devil did run and beg; I'll bet he won't come here again with his old horse pistol to shoot me. I guess that's fun enough for tonight, General, and you can go to bed now. I will come tomorrow night and show you another rascal in this crowd." Old Hickory was anxious to stay a week, but his party had enough of that thing. No one knew whose turn would come next, and no inducements could keep them. They spent the next night in Springfield, and returned to Nashville the following day.

There was much talk about the witch shaking hands with one of the Johnson's, a near neighbor, and Patrick McGowin, a highly esteemed Irishman, who lived across the line in Montgomery County, and had refused to shake hands with all other persons, for the reason, as was stated the witch said, thee two men were honest and truthful and could be trusted when they promised not to try to hold or squeeze its hand. I knew Mr. McGowen well, who was then getting to be quite an old man, and knew he was cautious, prudent and perfectly reliable in all he said. This was his general character, and I went to see him expressly to hear his own statement about the matter. We discussed the witch and the many mysterious stories in regard to the occurrences at Bell's, which he could in no way account for. I asked him particularly about the handshaking. The old gentleman talked about it with some reluctance. He said the witch did offer to shake hands with him, but he was not sure it could be called a handshaking. He held out his hand for that purpose, and felt something in his hand, which felt like a hairy substance. Calvin Johnson described that which he felt, like unto a woman's hand.

Dr. Henry Sugg was a man of great prominence in that community. He was quite a small boy during the reign of the witch, and of course never witnessed the early demonstration; and growing up skeptical, did not believe the stories told by the older people. He was disposed to ridicule the whole matter when spoken of, and he heard much about it in his practice among the sick. The old Bell house was torn down after the death of the old people, and moved to the place near Brown's ford, now owned by Levi Smith. It was also said that when the witch took its departure, it promised to return after a certain number of years and remain permanently, and this many people believed. This brings me to Dr. Sugg's statement which I had from his own lips. He was called to see a patient at this house, some thirty years after the witch first disappeared, or in the fifties. If I mistake not, he said Joel Bell lived there or owned the place. Anyway, the subject of the Bell Witch came up, and the man told about the strange noise heard and ridiculous things that had occurred the night before, and said he was sure that it was the Bell Witch. Dr. Sugg laughed at the man and told him it was all imagination, that the Bell Witch was a hoax and there never was anything in it, ridiculing his superstition. Just then he heard a terrible rattling of the vials in his medical bag, setting on the floor near the door, where he had placed the pocket as he entered the house, and immediately following the rattling noise came the sound of explosion, as if every bottle in the valise had burst or the corks all popped out. He rushed immediately to the pockets to see what had hap pened, and found everything intact, just as it should be. Then it was the other man's turn to ridicule him. He, however, tried to explain the phenomena to the satisfaction of the superstitious man, and while doing so the same sound was repeated with still greater force, and the second examination discovered nothing wrong or out of place in the valise, and, said he, "I could find no explanation for the mystery, and never have; it was so remarkable and unmistakable that there could be no explanation."

Mrs. Wimberly, who was a daughter of Mat. Ligon, told me about the visit of Betsy Bell to her father's on the occasion when the witch followed and abused her dreadfully, boxing her jaws, pinching her arms and pulling her hair, calling her ugly names, for trying to run away from it. Ligon's family got no rest that night, and were terribly frightened. I could tell you many other stories in regard to this unexplained mystery, but no doubt you have them all from the statement of Williams Bell and others.

—T. L. YANCEY

The house referred to by Col. Yancey is the same building in which Reynolds Powell and Allen Bell had a lively experience some time about 1861, as described in another chapter. The body of the house is made of hewed logs, now probably 100 years old, well preserved by weatherboarding.

# Chapter 12

## *Theny Thorn: Reminiscences from the Girl Who Associated Most with Betsy Bell*

Mrs. Lucinda E. Rawls, of Clarksville, Tenn., widow of the late J. J. Rawls, and daughter by the marriage of David Alexander Gooch and Partheny Thorn, contributes the following graphic interview from the reminiscences of her mother and other things connected with the exciting events of the Bell Witch history, and the effect and influence upon the community. Theny Thorn was born in 1803. Her parents lived in Stewart County, and died while she was quite a small child, too young to remember them. She was a niece of Jane Marvlin, who possessed considerable property, and became the second wife of James Johnson, father of John and Calvin by his first marriage. Mr. Johnson and second wife had no children, and they adopted Theny Thorn and raised her from a child, loving her as their own bestowing much care and devotion upon her, and she knew them only as father and mother, and Mrs. Rawls alluded to the old people most affectionately as grandfather and grandmother.

Mrs. Rawls very cheerfully granted this interview, and said she was willing to state anything she knew personally or that which she had heard repeated by her mother, Grandfather James Johnson, John and Calvin Johnson, Dr. Ardra Gooch, John Bell, Jr., and many others concerning the Bell Witch. It was, she says, a common subject of discussion in all family circles and neighborhood gatherings from her childhood up to the time she left the neighborhood in 1855, and she has rarely failed to hear the mystery spoken of on her visits to that vicinity since. "Yes," replied Mrs. Rawls, in answer to certain questions, "the Bell Witch was, and is still, a great scapegoat. Every circumstance out of the regular order of things is attributed to the witch. It has not been long since a man claiming to be the witch was waylaid and murdered by two men who were cleared, on the plea that the murdered man had bewitched them."

"Mother was very intimate with Betsy Bell," continued Mrs. Rawls, "and sympathized deeply with her in the trouble and affliction brought upon her by the wicked thing. It not only punished her severely, but frightened the poor girl almost out of her life, and mother stayed with her the more on this account to relieve her fears; in fact, her parents were afraid to leave her in her room alone a single night, and mother stayed with her almost every night, except when Becky Porter was there. It was very cruel in some people, she said, to charge the awful thing against Betsy. She was only twelve or thirteen years of age when the demonstrations commenced. She was a very tender, sweet girl, and was constantly under the gentle watch care of her mother, and never had an opportunity or any chance to learn such an art, if it were possible, and it was not in her nature to do so, nor could she have possibly escaped detection. Those who accused her could never state a reason or offer a shadow of evidence to that effect. The persecutions of the witch were enough for any frail mortal to bear, (more than her father could bear) without the slanderous charges of ignorant men who were incapable of discerning the cause, to crush her hope in life."

**Question**: Mrs. Rawls, did you ever hear your mother state in what particular way the witch annoyed Betsy?

**Answer**: "Yes, repeatedly; in every conceivable way and form imaginable. It would not let a bit of cover stay on the bed. It would pinch the girl till she would scream, slap her checks, pull her hair, stick pins in her body, and sometimes almost take her breath. Mother said it would seem to jerk the tucking comb out of her hair and dash it on the floor. You know that the girls in those days put up their hair with long tooth combs, instead of hair pins as now used. The combs were generally made of tortoise shell, which were ornamented and were pretty and costly, and easily broken by dropping on the floor, and strange as it appears, Mother said Betsy never had one broken, though they struck the floor as if thrown with force. Mother said she had seen this trick performed often when looking directly at Betsy, and knew she did not move her hands and no visible hand or cause could be detected. Betsy had a fine suit of long flaxen hair, which hung in beautiful waves that made her appear most charming, and she was very proud of it. When the tuckers were pulled out, her hair would drop all about her neck and shoulders and become so tangled that it would require a full half hour's time to comb it out. Then the witch would break out with hilarious laughter, 'Ha, ha, Betsy, if Josh could see you now he would envy me.' It carried on such mischief nearly all night, pulling the cover from the bed as fast as they could replace it, knocking over the chairs and keeping up a continual gabbing of nonsensical talk and laughter, and they were compelled to gas with the invisible thing through fear of something worse. Mother said she had spent many nights with no one else but Betsy and herself in the room, with doors and windows securely closed, and all efforts to detect the agency of these demonstrations or the source from whence came the remarkable voice, were in vain. Another favorite trick of the witch was that of tampering with Betsy's shoes. Mother said she had seen the strings tied so tight that the girl could not loose the knot, and the next minute the shoes would be unlaced and jerked from her feet. Sometimes when preparing to retire, the witch would exclaim, 'Betsy let me unlace your shoes and in a second her shoes would be pulled from her feet. Mother said she asked the witch why it would not unlace and remove her shoes, and the reply would come, 'I don't like you Theny, you are so silly; I don't want anything to do with you?'"

**Question**: Did you ever hear your mother repeat the circumstance of the four-leaf clover, which has been so generally spoken of?

**Answer**: "Yes, I have heard her tell it frequently to different persons. That occurred in this way. There were a number of young people in company, discussing the witch. Someone remarked that according to the saying, if any one could find a four-leaf clover they would be able to see the witch. Clover, you know, uniformly has three leaves, and it is very rare that four leaves are found. However, mother paid a visit to the Misses Pacely, daughters of Tanner Pacely, near Russellville, Ky. The girls were out one evening for a walk, and while strolling through a field, mother discovered a clover with four leaves, which she pulled, placing it in the front fold of her dress without calling any attention to it, intending carrying the clover home to try her luck, and not one discovered her action or purpose; nor did she mention the fact to a soul, lest people would think her superstitious, and silly. She returned home the next day with the clover in the bosom of her dress. It was late in the afternoon when she arrived, and very soon 'Kate,' as they called the witch, exclaimed, 'Lord Jesus, Theny, what a fool you have made of yourself; you went all the way to old man Pacely's to hunt a four leaf clover and brought It home secretly in your bosom, believing that it would enable you to see me, but you will never be smart enough for that, ha, ha, ha,' and so it went on teasing mother, and telling the joke to everyone who came in."

**Question**: Did the witch stay regularly at James Johnson's?

**Answer**: "No, it only visited grandfather's occasionally, as it did several other places. Grandfather was a very devout Christian, and a very zealous worker in the Methodist Church. He made it a rule through life to hold family worship before retiring at night, and often the neighbors would gather in and have prayer meetings at his house. The witch was generally present on such occasions, and during prayers would thump and scratch on the chairs and do other mischief, and would tell the folks at Bell's, 'I went to hear "Old Sugar Mouth" pray last night; Lord Jesus, how good he did get.' It called grandfather 'Old Sugar Mouth.' It also visited the family at other times, and would talk about any and everything, discuss the Scriptures, and gossip about the affairs of the country. Grand father said it seemed to know everything that was transpiring. Uncle John Johnson was at Mr. Bell's during the last day of the old gentleman's illness. I heard him tell the circumstances of finding a strange vial of medicine in the cupboard that no one could account for or tell what was in the vial. The witch said it put the vial there for Old Jack, and had given him a dose to kill him. There were several men present, who had called in to see Mr. Bell, and hearing this, someone advised John Bell, Jr., to test the medicine on a cat. He did so, giving the cat a very small portion, which threw it into convulsions instantly. The cat squalled, whirled around and died in a few minutes. Drew Bell had gone out before the vial was discovered, to direct the hands about some work on the place, and the first that Drew heard of the matter was from the witch. The very moment Drew returned, Kate commenced, 'Drew, John found that vial of medicine I put in the cupboard for Old Jack, and gave the cat some of it. Lord Jesus, how it did make that cat squall, jump up, turn over and die.'"

**Question**: Mrs. Rawls, did you ever hear your mother speak of the exploits of magicians or conjurers who came along?

**Answer**: "Yes, there were ever so many witch doctors during the time working incantations and magic arts, but with no avail. They were a great set of frauds. One or two I have in mind, and one who thought he had succeeded to a wonderful degree. One of these wizards notified the Bell family that he would be there on a cer tain day to kill the witch, and instructed that two silver dollars be concealed in a certain form or way, to make bullets, as he would be able to see the thing and shoot it with a silver bullet. The Bells tried everything suggested, no matter what it was, that looked to the discovery of the plague, and the money was hidden away in the cupboard as directed, and it was not suspected that the witch would know anything about it. The conjurer, however, failed to come, and Kate then told them all about the arrangement, laughing heartily, and told them that they had better take that money out of the cup-board and put it to some better use. On another occasion a witch doctor insisted that he could relieve Betsy of the spell if she would take his medicine, and she readily agreed to take his prescription. Mother remonstrated with Betsy against taking the awful dose, but she persisted that she would take any thing that anybody would give her, even if it was poison, to get rid of her excruciating pest, and so she did swallow it down. It very soon made her deathly sick, as the conjurer promised it would, and immediately a copious evacuation of the stomach followed. The excrement was examined and found to be literally full of pins and needles, and Kate, the witch, fairly roared with laughter, and said that fellow was the only conjurer who had ever done any good. He had made Betsy throw up pins and needles enough to supply the whole community, and if he would give her another dose of that stuff, he would get enough to set up a pin and needle store. The witch doctor really believed that the pins and needles were ejected from the girl's stomach, and was as-tounded by the result of his own practice. There could be no mis-take that they were real brass pins and needles. Mother gathered up a number and kept them as long: as she lived. I have seen the pins and needles myself. As a matter of course Betsy could not have lived with such a conglomeration in her stomach, and the only solution of the matter was that the witch dropped the pins and needles in the excrement unobserved; just as it pulled off her shoes, disheveled her hair, gave her and her mother hazelnuts, and many other miracu-lous performances that no one could ever account for."

**Question**: Mrs. Rawls, did you know Mrs. Kate Batts, or ever hear her name discussed in connection with the witchery?

**Answer**: "Yes, Mrs. Kate Batts lived many years after the death of John Bell and wife; after I was quite grown. She was very odd in her ways, original, having many funny sayings, and was the com-mon talk of the neighborhood. I remember that she caused me to get an awful scolding from father for laughing at her on a certain occasion. It was during a protracted meeting at Red River Church. Rev. Thomas Felts had concluded a revival sermon that aroused the entire audience, and had called up the mourners, who were kneel-ing at the front seat as usual, praying, when Mrs. Batts came in and spread her riding skirt over Joe Edwards, who was a mourner, and sat down on him. The scene was so ludicrous that I could not restrain myself, and with several other girls, we got into a great titter. The efforts of the brethren to get her up, her refusal to rise, and quaint expressions, made the matter worse, and the whole house burst into laughter. It was enough to make an angel laugh, and I just had to tell father that he was too sanctimonious for heaven. Mrs. Batts had but three children. Mary, her only daughter, was a beautiful girl, very sprightly and lovely. Her sons, both mature men, were quite to the contrary. John was married; Calvin tall and very awkward. Mrs. Batts thought Calvin the finest young man in the country, and had a peculiar way of introducing and commending him to society, by pushing her self into company, remarking, 'Girls, keep your eyes on Calvin; he is all warp ready for the filling.'"

"You ask me what people thought of Mrs. Batts in connection with the witchery. The truth is some people firmly believed that she was the witch, and was afraid of her. Seventy-five years ago people were not very distantly removed from the age of witchcraft. Educational facilities were limited. People relied on the country school teacher and the preacher, and as a matter of fact superstition was abroad in the land. People accepted the teaching of the Scriptures literally, and those familiar with the Bible could quote freely in support of the doctrine of witchcraft. The whole country was excited by the wonderful performances of the Bell Witch, and people unable to discover any cause or agency for such exhibitions, naturally attributed it to witchery, and there was no better scapegoat than Mrs. Kate Batts, because it fitted her character so well. The witch, in the first instance, gave out the information that it was 'Old Kate Batts' Witch.' It was said that John Bell had a misunderstanding with Mrs. Batts in some trading between them soon after he came to the country. Mrs. Batts got very mad, said hard things, and made threats that she would get even with him. Again it was said that Mrs. Batts was constantly on the pad from house to house, always wanting to buy wool rolls or sell something, and begged every woman she met with for a pin. These with many other circumstances led superstitious people to believe that she was a witch. Those who gave the matter intelligent consideration and investigation, though failing on every hypothesis for an explanation of the mystery, did not believe Mrs. Batts capable of performing such tricks. But to give you some idea of the extent and character of the superstition that prevailed, I will state two or three circumstances. The fact that Mrs. Batts was always begging pins was regarded as a direct circumstance against her, because the witch also had a weak ness for pins, and used them quite freely on Betsy Bell and the witch doctors, and pins were frequently found in the bed pillows, stuck from the inside of the pillow case with points out, and sometimes found in the chairs, and the saying was that the witch had power over any one who gave her pins. Again I remember, on the occasion of Mrs. Batts' death, the news soon spread all over the country, and it was difficult to find any lady who was willing to set up one night with the corpse, as was customary. Finally Fannie Sory volunteered to pay this respect to the dead if three or four other girls would join her and the company was then made up. After the burial next day, those girls told that they were beset with black cats and black dogs all night. One of them vowed to me that it was every word true, and she could prove it by the other girls. Two of the girls went to the well during the night for fresh water, and said they had to fight dogs with sticks all the way from the house to the well — large black curly haired dogs. The yard was full, while the house was full of black cats, constantly jumping on the coffin. This was undoubtedly a bit of wicked mischief on the part of the girls, practicing on the superstition of people, and many believed every word of it. Doubtless there were one or two black dogs belonging to the place, and like as many black cats, as cats and dogs were generally plentiful about every place. Another circumstance that occurred previous to the old lady's death: Emily Paine had the task of churning one morning. She was in a great hurry to get through, and after churning two hours, and the butter failing to come, her patience gave out, and she remarked that she just knew old Kate Batts had bewitched the milk, and she was going to burn her. She set the churn of milk aside and heated an iron poker red hot, and stuck it down in the churn, leaving it there, saying she was determined to find out if Mrs. Batts was burnt, and at once made some excuse for calling on the old lady. Sure enough Mrs. Batts was nursing a sore hand, which she said was burnt that morning. This confirmed the case beyond a doubt. I have heard Mrs. Paine, Emily's mother, tell this story and laugh. Emily Paine afterwards married Henry Calhoon."

## The Murder

The murder referred to by Mrs. Rawls was the killing of a man named Smith, by Thomas Clinard and Richard Burgess; which occurred at a railroad crossing, between Springfield and Cedar Hill about 1875 or '76. Smith came into the community a stranger, and was employed by Mr. Fletcher, where Clinard and Burgess were also engaged on the farm. Smith professed to be something of a wizard, or rather boasted of his power to hypnotize and lay spells on people, subjecting any one who came under his influence to his will, and it was reported that he claimed to have de rived this power from the mantle of the Bell Witch. However, the writer interviewed Hon. John F. House, who was council for the defense, on the subject, who says that no such evidence was produced in the trial, but that the lawyers handled the Bell Witch affair for all that it was worth in the defense of their clients, presenting the analogy or similarity of circumstances with good effect on the jury. The evidence was overwhelming to the effect that Smith did practice hypnotism or some such art on the defendants, and had them completely under his control and practiced on their fears with dire threats, and made the them do many foolish things that they detested, and they could not escape his dogging influence that subjected them to ridicule. They tried to evade and shun Smith, and for this he chided and threatened them; consequently the animosity, and they planed his murder and waylaid and shot him to death, and then surrendered to the legal authorities, standing trial on a plea of self-defense and were cleared. It was one of the most interesting cases that ever came before the courts of this country, and the entire community acquiesced in the decision of the court. No doubt that the young men owe their escape from the fearful rigor of the law to the powerful pleadings and matchless eloquence of Col. House, who has so often distinguished himself as a great orator, lawyer and philanthropist.

# Chapter 13

## *Recollections: How the Hon. John D. Tyler Visited the Witch*

Having heard the name of Hon. John D. Tyler mentioned as one of the investigators, the writer called on Judge Charles W. Tyler, of Clarksville, Tenn., to know if he ever heard his distinguished father speak of the mystery.

"Yes," said he, "I have heard my father tell many wonderful things that occurred at Bell's about the time he moved to this county from Virginia. I remember that he said reports concerning the mysterious affair reached Virginia before he left that State, and his friends laughed and ridiculed him for moving to a haunted country. But of course he paid no attention to such jeers and jests, for he did not believe the story. But when he arrived here, which was in the Fall of 1818, he found great excitement prevailing all over the country and he joined in with others, visiting the place to investigate the cause. I shall not undertake to detail any statements that my father made in regard to what he saw and heard on these occasions; but you can refer to me for the fact that he did state that he investigated the matter to his full satisfaction; having entered upon the investigation deeply impressed that the demonstrations were made by members of the family, and he pursued his inquiry along this line, making every test possible, and became thoroughly convinced that no member of the family had anything to do with it, and further than that, the mystery to him was never solved.

Judge Tyler is so well known in Tennessee, that the mention of his name is sufficient for home people. But for the information of those in other sections, we will state that he is a citizen of Clarksville, Tenn., County Financier, and Judge of the County and Criminal Court, which positions he has held eighteen years by the suffrage of the people. His father, Hon. John D. Tyler, was one of the most eminent educators known in this country in early days. He served one or two terms in the State Senate, and was prominent in all public affairs, as he was widely known as a man of high intelligence, and distinguished for his thoroughness in everything he undertook. There is no question that he entered upon the investigation with the determination to discover the cause if possible, but gave it up after satisfying himself of his mistake regarding the connection of any member of the family with the affair.

# Mrs. Mahala Darden's Minute Description of John Bell — His Strange Affliction — Betsy Bell and Joshua Gardner Were Lovers

The writer made a special visit during July, 1892, to Cedar Hill, Tenn., for the purpose of interviewing Mrs. Mahala Darden, one of the most estimable ladies of Robertson county, then eighty-five of age. Mrs. Darden resides with her son, Charles Darden, a prosperous farmer, two miles from Cedar Hill. She is the pride and delight of the family, and a mother to be proud of. Mrs. Darden retains to a remarkable degree her physi cal strength and activity, while her memory is so clear and bright that she details incidents of her girlhood with the greatest accuracy, giving dates and circumstances, and altogether she is one of the most intelligent and entertaining ladies in the county, loved and venerated as mother by the entire community. After some pleasant conversation, the subject of the Bell Witch was broached.

"Yes," replied the good lady, "I have a very distinct recollection of the prevailing excitement during, the witch period. There never was any thing like it; people talked about nothing else, and a great many went to hear it; Mr. Bell's house was full of people almost constantly."

Did you witness any of the witch demonstrations, Mrs. Darden? "Oh, no; I was rather too young. Parents did not think it prudent to take their children, especially girls. Moreover, I had no desire to go at that time."

Will you tell what you know about John Bell and his family, and all about the witch, as you heard the story from the old people? "Certainly. John Bell was a fine looking gentleman, a man of distinguished appearance, and was one of the wealthiest men in the country. He always had plenty of money, and was very prosperous. He was also popular and highly respected by the people. I remember distinctly the first time I ever saw Mr. Bell, and how he impressed me. It was in 1817. My father, James Byrns, was a magistrate, living then several miles from John Bell's. Mr. Bell came to my father's one day with quite a number of men to attend a trial or some law business before my father. His commanding appearance was so marked as to distinguish him over all others, and impress me with his presence. I was then ten years old, and had learned to spin. Work was creditable to a girl in those days, and especially was it a mark of distinction for one of my years to become an expert in handling the cards and spinning wheel, and I was very proud of it. Well, I had the wheel out in the middle of the floor, making it fairly whiz. I had set in for a big day's work, expecting much praise from mother at night, and the men soon crowded the house so full that father told me I would have to move my wheel out and give up the spinning. I did so, and went to help mother about other things. Dinner was prepared for the company, and when I went in to notify father that dinner was ready, I noticed that all rose up for the invitation except Mr. Bell, who shook his head declining. Father extended him the second invitation, which he still declined, shaking his head. Some remarks were made at the table about his refusal. He seemed depressed, confused and sullen. Mr. Bell returned on the following day, riding four or five miles, telling father that he came expressly to apologize and explain his conduct on the previous day, lest he (my father) should take offence for his refusal to dine. 'All of a sudden,' said he, 'my tongue became strangely affected. Some thing that felt like a fungus growth came on both sides, pressing against my jaws, filling my mouth so that I could not eat or talk.' It was said that Mr. Bell was affected in this way off and on to his death. Nothing, however, was known at this time of the Bell witch trouble; at least, was not known outside of the family. Soon after this my father moved to a farm near Mr. Bell's, and the two families became intimate. The first I heard of the witch, was told as a secret, said to have leaked out through young John Bell, who told an intimate friend that something strange and very troublesome was disturbing the family. I was about twelve years old when the witch excitement reached its highest tension. My father went frequently to witness the mystery. The first time he heard it, the noise was like that of ducks fluttering and washing in a pond of water. He described many strange things which occurred after that. Mrs. Lucy Bell told me about the witch bringing her grapes and hazelnuts, and emptying the sugar out of the bowl on the hearth, and many other things. They were wonderful tricks, but I could not disbelieve Mrs. Bell. David Darden said he determined in his own mind one night to outdo the witch. He wrapped the cover of his bed around his hand, and held with all his might, but the witch stripped the bed in spite of him. When it visited Mr. Porter's it made a noise like a log of wood falling on the house. The witch told at Mr. Bells that it intended visiting every family in the neighborhood, and did visit many as reported, but never came to my father's that I know of, and I was in constant dread, fearing it would come. Mrs. Bartlett said she was there one night when many persons were waiting to hear the witch talk. Finally a rapping or noise was heard just outside, and several went to the door to see what it was, when the witch laughed out, exclaiming, 'Oh it's nothing but Old Caesar lapping out of the bath tub.' Old Caesar was the dog. I heard a good deal of laughter about a trick it played on Drew Bell. Drew leaned his chair back against the bureau, which set against the wall, placing his feet on the rounds. Instantly the bureau was snatched from behind him and Drew tumbled down on the floor. The witch told him to get up, that he ought to have better sense than lean against the bureau. On one occasion a little unknown black dog came to the house, cutting some antics. Mr. Bell said he would shoot that dog, and started to get his gun. Mrs. Bell interfered, telling him he must not. The dog lay down on the floor and rolled over and over toward the door, and the minute the dog disappeared from the house the witch exclaimed, 'Look out, Old Jack, here comes Jerusalem.'"

Did you know Rev. Thomas and Rev. James Gunn, Mrs. Darden? "Indeed I did. They were the founders of Methodism in this community. Two nobler ministers never lived in this section, and I have never seen two men imbued with more spirituality, and have never heard any preacher with more inspiration. They preached all over the country for many miles around, after going a whole day's journey or more, and great revivals resulted from their preaching."

Did they visit Mr. Bell's or try to detect the witch? "My understanding was at the time that they did. Mr. Bell sent for them often and they tried faithfully to throw some light upon the mystery, but never could."

Did you know the Batts family? "Yes; there were two Batts families. Quite a number of the descendents of Jerry Batts are still living here, and they are mighty fine people. The other Batts family, descendants of Fred and Kate Batts, have disappeared."

What do you know, Mrs. Darden, of Mrs. Kate Batts? "Oh, Aunt Kate, as the young people all called her, was a good kind hearted old lady. She was very peculiar in her ways, and was mighty funny, which made people talk about her a great deal. But I always liked Aunt Kate, she was so cheerful and full of life I was glad to meet her. She was very sensitive. The witch told someone that it was 'Old Kate Batts,' and this is why the witch took the name of Kate. Some people were silly enough to believe it. She heard this and it made her very mad. She turned loose her tongue on people who talked about her in a way that made some really afraid of her. I did not blame her for getting mad at such foolishness. Of course she was no witch; if she had been she would have bewitched everyone who talked bad about her. The witch gave itself many names, called itself Black Dog, Jerusalem and other names. People discussed all of these things, watched Mrs. Batts, and tried every way to detect the cause, but no discovery that I ever heard of that threw the least suspicion on Aunt Kate beyond the simple statement of the witch, which as a matter of course was false and intended to mislead. You know how people fly to extremes and jump at conclusions when trying to unravel or penetrate a great mystery. Some charged that it was John and Drew Bell practicing ventrilo quism. Others thought it was Betsy Bell practicing some unknown art, but the more sensible people accepted none of these theories; in fact they would not support any kind of investigation. What on earth could possibly have induced the Bells to inflict so much distress and punishment on the family, even had they the power? Not money, for they had that, and refused to receive a cent from the many strangers and in vestigators calling. Not notoriety, for they kept the whole matter a secret as long as possible. Then it could not add anything to the good name Mr. Bell had earned for himself and family and cherished so much. No, it was simply a phenomenon which no one could explain."

Did you ever hear Jerry Batts express his opinion about the witch? "Yes; he discussed it a great deal with father and mother in my presence, but they never arrived at any satisfactory explanation. I remember distinctly one expres sion from Mr. Jerry Batts that impressed me. He remarked to father, 'The witch will never leave until John Bell's head is cut off,' meaning of course, not as long as the old gentleman lived. I suppose it was Mr. Bell's peculiar afflictions that led him to make the remark. The witch had declared its intention to kill him, and the old gentleman charged his affliction to that source. The witch did torment him to his grave, and reviled with ghoulish glee at his burying. A large crowd of people attended the funeral, and it was a very solemn occasion — everyone seemed sadly depressed. After the grave was filled and the crowd of sorrowing friends started to leave, the witch commenced singing:

'Row me up some brandy, O,
  Row row, row row,
Row me up some brandy, O,
  Row me up some more.'"

Did you know Joshua Gardner, Mrs. Darden? "Yes. He was Betsy Bell's lover at the time, and it was generally believed that the sentiment was mutual. Betsy thought much of him. He came of a splendid family of people, was a handsome young man, full six feet tall, and weighed about one hundred and sixty pounds. He had dark hair and gray eyes, was intelligent and entertaining, and a man of good deportment, and very popular in the community."

Please, Mrs. Darden, describe Betsy Bell? "Betsy was a beautiful girl. She was of light complexion; what you would call a blonde. She was a little above medium height, presenting a graceful figure and elegant carriage. She possessed a rare suit of rich golden hair, soft gentle blue eyes and winning ways, and with all was an industrious, bright and interesting girl, who had more admirers than any girl in the country. I thought a great deal of Betsy; she was a sweet good girl, and I deeply sympathized with her in her disappointments and afflictions."

Then Betsy did not marry young Joshua Gardner? "No; she finally married Richard Powell, her school teacher, who was a very prominent man."

Do you know; Mrs. Darden, what broke up the love affair between Betsy and Gardner, and induced her to marry Powell? "Ah, now you ask me a hard question; I cannot tell. You may learn that from others. It was said that the witch had something to do with it but I do not know. I always thought Betsy loved Gardner best, that is she seemed happy in his company, and he was certainly greatly devoted to her when out in society. You know, however, that it has always been said that destiny controls the fortunes of men and women. You know also that women are counted as very fickle creatures, and there is no accounting for the change of a woman's mind in love affairs, and often the most desperate love cases come to naught. Don't you think I have told you enough?"

"Yes, Mrs. Darden, many thanks for this very entertaining interview."

## Rev. James G. Byrns's Statements — First Appearance of the Witch — Its Doings qnd Sayings — The Witch Killer from The East

Rev. James G. Byrns, one of the oldest and most highly esteemed citizens of Springfield, Tenn., a man whose years are full of good works, and whose integrity is above reproach of any kind, contributes the following interesting sketch, which goes to establish the character of the witnesses, giving a graphic account of the first appearance of the witch and its operations. The writer of this sketch is a son of Squire James Byrns, who was the good magistrate of the Bell district, a man of high moral character, noted for his intelligence and general usefulness as a citizen, and his impartiality and faithfulness in the dis charge of his official duties. Mr. Byrns, being requested to prepare a sketch, writes as follows:

Of course I am too young to know anything personally about the Bell Witch, but shall endeavor to state faithfully some of the facts impressed upon me, as I have so often heard them detailed by my father, James Byrns, Sr., John Johnson, Calvin Johnson, Alex Gunn, Sr., William Porter, Frank R. Miles, Martin Pitman, Mrs. Rebecca Long, my wife's mother, who was Rebecca Porter, Mrs. Martha Bell, and many other citizens, and have also heard many miraculous statements by Negroes, which I will not repeat.

Old Mr. Bell told my father, also John Johnson and others, that the first unaccountable object that attracted his attention was a large, strange looking animal, resembling a dog. He walked out to the field to see if the fodder was ripe enough to gather. Before starting he cleaned his gun and loaded it to shoot squirrels and rabbits around the field. About the middle of the field, he said, he discovered the animal sitting in the row, looking intently at him. He approached nearer to it, and the dog, as he thought it was, did not move, which surprised him, and he then concluded to shoot it. At the fire of the gun the strange looking creature ran, and as soon as it moved, he discovered that it was an uncommon animal, and knew there was no dog in the country like it. However, this circumstance was without significance, and was forgotten until later developments connected it with other affairs.

Soon after this the trouble commenced. Something appeared scratching on the outside wall of the house, and occasionally a tap at the door. Mr. Bell said he frequently went out to see what was the matter, but could discover nothing. He said nothing about it, not even to the family, lest it might alarm them, and thinking too that it was someone playing pranks, and by watching he would be able to discover the intruder. Such demonstrations continued to increase, being heard two or three times during a week, and become so intolerable that Mr. Bell determined to lay some scheme to catch the offender. Finally the mysterious knocking appeared to be within the upper story of the house, and sometimes the noise would appear like trace chains or harness falling on the floor above him, but on investigation nothing could be found. From this on the demonstrations increased, and appeared like rats gnawing and dogs fighting in the house. After carrying on at this rate for some time, it commenced troubling various members of the family, pulling the covers off of the beds, pinching and slapping the children, and became so frightful that the family could no longer conceal their distress, and neighbors were called in to witness the strange occurrences and detect the cause. But no one to this day has been able to explain or account for the mystery. The more people investigated, the more demonstrative it became, sounds like heavy stones and chunks of wood falling on the floor being heard. Finally the witch commenced talking and laughing, singing and praying. For some time it was very pious, and later became extremely wicked, using unchaste and most offensive language. The mystery deepened, and everyone who undertook to explain it was covered with confusion. Some people thought it was two members of the Bell family practicing ventriloquism, but this theory soon exploded, by applying the strictest tests. The reader will remember that I am stating these things just as they were detailed to me by the parties above named, who were witnesses all through the troubles. The witch talked more freely to some parties than to others. It seemed to prefer talking with John Johnson and Bennett Porter more than any other persons, perhaps because they were more disposed to humor and gab with it than were others, Bennett Porter was Mr. Bell's son-in-law — married Esther Bell. The witch promised him one night to go home with him that the family might have some rest. Then it said, "Bennett, you will try to kill me if I visit your house."

"No I won't," replied Porter. ",Oh, but I know you," replied the witch, "but I have been to your house. Do you remember that bird you thought sung so sweet the other morning?"

"Yes," replied Porter. "Well that was me." Then continued the witch, "Bennett, didn't you see the biggest and poorest old rabbit that you ever saw in your life, as you came over here this evening?"

"Yes," replied Mr. Porter. "Well that was me," said the witch, and who then burst into laughter. This was the kind of gossip it carried on constantly, and would tell what different people in the neighborhood had been doing during the day, or what was then transpiring.

It seemed to take special delight in afflicting and tormenting old Mr. Bell, and his young daughter Betsy. It often said that it had come to kill old Jack Bell and it was said that Mr. Bell died from strange afflictions visited on him by his tormentor. It interfered a great deal with Betsy's love affairs, and wanted her to marry a certain man in the neighborhood. Betsy complained of a painful, sensation like someone sticking pins in her body. It would fill her hair full of pins, jerk her tucking comb out, and laugh at its own wicked tricks and Betsy's discomfiture, and she was frequently sent from home for rest and freedom from the tortures inflicted by the witch.

It was very common for large crowds to gather at Mr. Bell's to hear the witch talk. One night when the house was full, there came an old gentleman by the name of Grizzard. The witch entered with the exclamation, "Here is old Grizzard; you all just ought to hear old Grizzard call his hogs. He begins, 'Pig, pig, pig.' The hogs come in a run, and Griz counts them and then begins hollering, 'Here, here, sic, sic, sowey, sowey.'

That's the way old Grizzard feeds his hogs." And Mr. Grizzard said the witch was correct. Next came the exclamation or inquiry, "Where is Jerusalem?" (Jerusalem was a member of the witch family.) No one replying, the same voice answered, "There he is on the wall." All eyes were at once turned to discover a large black bug crawling on the wall. Mr. Bell remarked, "Well, if that is Jerusalem, I will kill him," and he did kill the bug. The witch laughed heartily, exclaiming, "Lord Jesus, what a fool I did make of old Jack Bell."

The Witch seemed to like old Mrs. Lucy Bell. It called her "Old Luce," and said Old Luce was a good woman, which was indeed her character throughout the country. Mrs. Bell had quite a spell of sickness, and one morning refused her breakfast. Very soon Mrs. Bell heard a soft pathetic voice, apparently just above her head, calling her name, "Luce, poor Luce, are you sick Luce?"

"Yes," replied Mrs. Bell, "I am."

"Well Luce, hold out your hands, and I will give you some hazelnuts I brought from the bottom; they will be good for you." Mrs. Bell held out her hands and received the hazelnuts as they dropped. Presently the same voice inquired, "Luce, poor Luce, why don't you eat the hazelnuts?"

"Oh, you know that I can't crack them," replied Mrs. Bell. Then it told her to hold out her hands again, saying, "I will crack some for you." Instantly the sound of the cracking was heard, and the cracked nuts were dropped on her lap. Several ladies were there ministering to Mrs. Bell, and testified to this. That night the witch came in with the news that a baby had just been born to a family living in the bottom, which proved to be correct as stated. I understand that the baby was Mrs. Wash. Ayers, now living. The next day it visited Mrs. Bell again, bringing a bunch of wild grapes in the same manner as the hazelnuts came.

On another occasion the witch came in a jolly good mood, when quite a number of persons were sitting in the room engaged in social intercourse, announcing its presence with the inquiry, "Who wants some grapes," and that moment a bunch of large wild grapes dropped in Betsy Bell's lap. I heard John Bell, Jr., and others confirm this circumstance.

Calvin Johnson told me that after some persuasion the witch consented to shake hands with him if he would promise not to catch it. He promised and held out his hand, and instantly felt something like a soft delicate hand resting on his. The hand was placed lengthwise on his, so that he could not grasp it. John Johnson asked, the witch why it would not shake hands with him? The answer was, "You are a rascal, Jack; you want to catch me." John said that was just what he intended to do. The witch seemed to have more confidence in Calvin Johnson than any one. It said Calvin was an honest man, truthful and free from deceit, and this was true of the man.

John Johnson called in one night when the witch was in a great way talking, and addressing the witch said, "Well Kate, you can't tell what my wife has been doing to-day?"

"Yes I can," it promptly replied, "she has been baking cakes for you to carry along to eat on your trip to Nashville, where you intend starting tomorrow." This Mr. Johnson said was true, and no one outside of the family could have known it.

One night someone inquired of the witch what was going on over at Jesse Bells? "I don't know,'" it answered, "but will go and see." Five minutes later the witch returned and told what every member of the family was doing at that hour, which was confirmed the next day by Jesse Bell.

During the excitement the conjurers and experts in divining mysteries came along, and of course the Bell family were disposed to let them try their experiments. One of these was a smart fellow from the East, who claimed to be a witch killer, and said he could, by some sort of divination, see witches and shoot them. This smart gentleman conjured around several days with hair balls and foxfire, washed out his gun with his charm mixture, molded silver bullets and loaded for the witch, and set around day after day waiting for the goblin to put in its appearance, but Kate did not show up. He said the witch was afraid of him and would not come as long as he remained. The family had almost arrived at the conclusion that there was something in the man, and Mr. Bell was seriously contemplating the wisdom of hiring the gentleman from the East to stay about to keep the witch away. The family had not enjoyed so long a respite since the specter's first appeared. Finally the witch killer concluded that he would go home, and return very soon to stay longer, should Kate make any more trouble. But he was firmly impressed that nothing more would be heard of it. His horse was brought to the front near the house, the witch man placed his saddle bags, stuffed with all kinds of conjurations, on the saddle, and bidding good-bye to Mr. Bell, the family and friends who came out to see him off, he mounted his horse to start, but the animal would not budge. He kicked, spurred and whipped, but it was no go. The horse would rear up, fall down and roll and kick. The witch man then turned to conjuring his horse, rubbed and petted the animal until it became quiet, and then mounted again, but the horse still refused to go. The witch killer was about to give up in despair, when the familiar voice of Kate was heard in the air, exclaiming, "I can make that horse go. Let me get on behind." Just then the horse dashed off, seemingly of its own accord, making a circle around the yard, kicking and squealing with wild rage, and the witch hollering, "Hold on old man, hold on." Finally the horse struck a bee line for the gate, and out he went, kicking and snorting, the rider hanging to the mane of the horse's neck, yelling for dear life, "Oh mercy." It appeared, however, that it was "Kate" and not mercy that had him. The witch laughed a week over that transaction. "Lord Jesus," it said, "I scared that old man nearly to death. I stuck him full of brass pins. He will spit brass pins and foxfire for the next six months. Lord Jesus, how he did beg. I told the old scoundrel that he came here to kill me, and I was not going to let him off easy. He said if I would let him alone he never would come here again. I broke him from trying that caper any more."

The witch told various stories concerning itself, and said it could be anything, assume any form it desired; a dog, a rabbit, bird, or human form. It finally told the family that if Betsy would marry a certain gentleman, it would leave and not trouble them any more. The Negroes could tell the most wonderful stories, and narrate miraculous escapes.

The men and women whom I have mentioned as my authority for this statement are all dead, but their memories live and speak for their integrity and veracity. They were as pure and truthful people as I ever knew, and strange and mysterious as the story of the Bell Witch may seem, I could not, if I would, doubt the statements of these people. As to what it was, or who it was, I cannot form or express any opinion, but as to the truth of the trouble, I have not the shadow of a doubt. The evidence that James Byrns, Sr. was my father, is not to me a particle stronger or more convincing. There is no court in all of the land that would require one-half of the testimony to establish any fact, as can be produced in support of the story of these wonderful demonstrations, rather I should say history, for in fact it is a part of the early history of Robertson county, and will be handed down from generation to generation in this county, just as stirring events that transpired at the building of Solomon's Temple have come down through a certain channel to the present time. Like the queen of Sheba when she heard the fame of Solomon concerning the name of the Lord, she came to prove him with hard questions, and confessed that the half had not been told her, people came from all quarters to see with their own eyes, or rather, hear with their own ears, and prove what they believed a cheap fraud and deception, but returned worse confounded than ever. Though Mr. Bell was a man in good prosperous circumstances, strangers and visitors who came on the mission of divining the mystery almost ate him out of house and home. In conclusion, therefore, I must confess with the testimony before me, I believe as firmly as I can believe anything that I have not seen or felt, the truth of the existence of the Bell Witch.

JAMES G. BYRNS.

## Some Thrilling Incidents Told by Mrs. Nancy Ayers, the Baby the Witch Spanked

Washington Ayers and wife are two happy old people living some two miles from the old Bell place, and about the same distance from Cedar Hill, Tenn. Mrs. Nancy Ayres is a daughter of John and Patsy Johnson, who had a most thrilling experience in trying to detect the authorship of the demoniac exhibitions, which disturbed the Bell family. She was born in 1819, and is still a very active lady for one at her ripe age. She is also intelligent and very entertaining, especially in describing the sensation which the Bell Witch left behind to live after the intensely exciting events of that period. Mrs. Ayres is greatly esteemed in the community. She inherited that rugged honesty which characterized the Johnson family, and is affectionately called "Aunt Nancy" by everyone. The writer was told before visiting Mrs. Ayers, "You can rely on everything Aunt Nancy says as strictly correct."

**Mrs. Ayers was asked if she was willing to tell all she knew about the Bell Witch?**

"Oh no, I could not tell the half I have heard in a week; strictly speaking, I know nothing. I was born in the middle of the most exciting events, and they say that the witch was the first to carry the news of my birth to the Bell family. All I know is hearsay from father, mother, Grandfather James Johnson, Uncle Calvin Johnson, Joel Bell, and everybody who lived in the neighborhood at that time, and, of course, I believe their statements as firmly as if I had witnessed the demonstrations."

*It is said that the witch whipped you when a baby. How is that, Mrs. Ayers?*

"Well, that is what father and mother told me repeatedly after I had grown up. It occurred in this way: Betsy Bell frequently came to our house to spend the night and get some rest if possible from the witch. In fact, father invited and urged her to come. He said he had two purposes in view; one was a desire to render any services possible that would relieve the family of the pest: even for a short time. His second reason was a determination to follow up every clue, or every line of investigation, that had been suggested or could be thought of, in an effort to elucidate the mystery. This he was doing on his own account and in his own way, and proceeded in a way to elude all suspicion of his purpose. Several persons who had been trying the detect to cause of the remarkable exhibitions and failing, had arrived at the conclusion that Betsy Bell possessed some extraordinary gift akin to ventriloquism, and was practicing a deception in collusion with some other person, and that he had about arrived at this conclusion himself, but carefully concealed his convictions from her and all other persons, and he thought he would have a better opportunity of determining this matter if she were to come alone to spend a few nights at his house. As before stated, she did come, and the witch came with her, keeping up so much talking, scratching, knocking over the chairs, pulling the covering from the beds, and other vexatious disturbances that it was impossible for any one to sleep while it was there, and this all went to confirm his opinion. So it happened one night when Betsy and the witch were there, that I was fretful and worried mother a great deal, she having to get up frequently to rock my cradle. Finally Kate, as they called the witch, spoke factiously, inquiring of mother, 'Patsy, why don't you slap that child and make it behave itself? If you won't I will.' Instantly they heard something like a hand spanking me, and I yelled to the top of my voice, as if something was taking my life, when both father and mother sprang out of bed to my rescue. They searched the room all over, but could find nothing irregular, no persons but themselves in the room, and no possible way that anyone .could have gotten in and out without a noise or detection."

*Did you behave after that?*

"Well, they said I did behave like a little lady the balance of the night."

*Did your father's investigations satisfy him thoroughly that Betsy Bell was culpable in the witch demonstration?*

"Oh no. To the contrary he became thoroughly satisfied that Betsy was entirely innocent of the whole matter, and was a great sufferer from the affliction, as was her father. It was said by those who had been watching Betsy, that the witch never talked when her lips were closed. This was not true. He said it talked to him not only when her lips were closed, but when she was not near, not in talking or hearing distance, and in fact would talk at old man Bell's when neither Betsy, Drew or young John were on the place, and yet seemed to follow Betsy wherever she went, going with her to grandfather's, James Johnson, when she visited Theny Thorn, and at bedtime go through the form of reading a chapter in the Bible, singing grandfather's favorite song, and offer prayer, just as he would. Father said it did many things that would have been impossible for a young girl like Betsy, and told things that she could not possibly have known. The witch talked almost incessantly, gabbing and spouting about everything that was going on in the country, seemed familiar with everybody's business, telling things that no one present knew anything about, called strangers by name and telling where they were from before they could introduce themselves. It would also quote Scripture, discuss doctrinal questions, sing songs, and pray eloquent prayers, and never failed to answer any question concerning any passage, verse or text in the Bible correctly, giving full references as to where it might be found. Then on the other hand it could be very wicked and out curse a sailor. Mr. Bell sometimes sent for father to set up and entertain Kate, that the family might get a little rest. He rather liked this, as it afforded him a better opportunity for prosecuting his investigations. The witch also seemed to like gossiping with him, and there was a peculiar excitement about it that interested him, and he would sit and talk to the thing just as patiently and earnestly as if he was discussing a very important matter with some person. Father said that one night after the witch had gone on for some time prattling about everything in the country, he concluded to change the topic and lead it out concerning itself, and beginning with flattery he said, 'Kate, I love to talk with you because you are so smart and can always learn me something. You and I have been good friends, and I want to know more about you. Now there is no person present but you and I; tell me confidentially something about yourself?' 'No Jack,' was the reply, 'I can't tell you that yet, but I will tell you before I leave.' 'How long before you will leave?' 'I won't tell you that neither, but I will not leave as long as old Jack Bell lives.' 'Have you really come to kill old Jack?' 'Yes, I have told him so over and often.' 'What has old Jack done that you want to kill him?' 'Oh, nothing particular; I just don't like him.' 'But everybody in the country likes him and regards him as a very fine old gentleman, don't they?' 'Yes, and that is the reason he needs killing.' 'But Kate, if you kill old Jack without giving a better reason than that, people will think very hard of you, and then according to law you will be hung for murder, won't you?' 'No, it's catching before hanging.' 'Yes, but isn't the maxim, "murder will out" equally true?' 'That may be Jack, but still its catching before hanging.' 'Well Kate, tell me why you hate Betsy; isn't she a sweet lovely girl?' 'How do you know Jack, that I hate Betsy?' 'Because you are always following and ding-donging after her.' 'Well, is that any evidence that I hate her?' 'But then you pull her hair, pinch her arms, stick pins in her.' 'Well, don't lovers play with each other that way sometimes?' 'No, I never did; no man who really loves a girl will serve her as you do Betsy.' 'How do you know that I am a man?' 'Because you get drunk and curse sometimes, and say and do things that no nice woman would do.' 'But Jack, why should I be a woman; may I not be a spirit or something else?' 'No Kate, you are no spirit. A spirit can't pull the cover from beds, slap people, pull hair, stick pins, scratch, and do such things like you.' 'Well, I will make you think I am a spirit before you get home.' 'How are you going to do that, Kate?' 'I am going to scare you.' 'You can't scare me, Kate; I know that you are too good a friend to do me any harm, and therefore I am not afraid of you.' 'Well, just wait until you start through the woods home, and see if I don't make you hump yourself.' 'Oh pshaw, Kate, you are just joking and gabbing now. Tell me where you live, and who and what you are, anyhow?' 'I live in the woods, in the air, in the water, in houses with people; I live in heaven and in hell; I am all things and anything I want to be; now don't you know what I am?' 'No, I don't; come and shake hands with me like you did with Calvin.' 'No, I can't trust you, Jack.' 'Why Kate, you trusted my brother Calvin and I am just as good as he is?' 'No you are not,' returned Kate, 'Calvin is a good Christian and a true man; he won't violate his promise for anything.' 'Neither will I.' 'Oh, but you are lying, Jack; I know you too well. You are smarter than Calvin, but you are a grand rascal, old Jack Johnson. You just want a chance to catch me; that is what you are here for, trying to find out who or what I am, and you want a chance to grasp my hand.' After much talking on this line, the conversation ended some time after midnight, and father started home. Kate never would shake hands with him, though he importuned often, nor did he ever learn anything more about the witch than was manifested in this conversation, which I have heard him repeat so often that I remember it word by word. Father said as soon as he reached the woods, the bushes and trees commenced cracking, like they were all breaking down, and sticks and chunks of wood fell about him thick and fast, as if thrown by someone. He never would acknowledge that he run, but I always believed he did. Father said the witch seemed to know his mind and purpose as well as he did himself, and that he was fully determined to try to catch it by the hand if it had shaken hands with him."

*Did you ever hear Calvin Johnson say it shook hands with him?*

"Yes, I have heard Uncle Calvin make the statement frequently. He said the Witch made him promise not to grasp or squeeze its hand before it consented, and he could not violate his Promise. He said he held out his hand, and very quick felt the pressure of' another hand on his, which was laid lengthwise, and not across, in the common form of shaking hands, and that it felt very soft, like a woman's hand. But it never would trust father, though it showed a preference for talking with him. It told others as it told him, that old Jack Johnson was smart and cunning, that he was a grand rascal, always hatching plans and schemes to catch it, and he had to be watched."

*Mrs. Ayres, your father, you say, addressed the witch as "Kate," did you ever hear him explain how it came by that name?*

"Yes; people continued their expostulations with overtures and importunities to reveal its name, purpose, etc. The witch had given many names and various explanations of its presence, but the biggest sensation of all came when it told that it was old Kate Batts' witch. Mrs. Batts was a very sensitive, peculiar, blustering kind of woman, whose eccentricities subjected her to much ridicule, and her original oddity was a kind of jesting stock, and common talk. So it was a popular hit, and started fresh gossip for all laughing tongues. It made the old lady very mad; she cut tall capers and said more funny things in her maledictions and imprecations than was ever heard, and naturally everybody took to calling the witch 'Kate.'"

*Did anybody really believe that Mrs. Kate Batts was the witch?*

"Yes, some people did, and they were afraid of her. Father said the idea was the most absurd and preposterous that had been advanced; contrary to all reason. Mrs. Batts, he said could not have had any conception of such a thing, much less practice the art, eluding detection. On another occasion father said he was postulating with Kate, begging the witch to tell something about itself. Kate replied, 'Well Jack, if you will agree to keep it a secret, and not tell old "Sugar Mouth," (that was. grandfather) I will tell you.' Of course father agreed to that. 'Now,' says Kate, 'I am your stepmother.' Father replied, 'Kate, you know you are lying; my stepmother is a good woman, and the best friend I have. She would not do so many mean things as you are guilty of.' 'Now,' replied Kate, 'I can prove it to you.' Grandmother Johnson had an unruly servant who would go wrong, irritating her very much, and the old lady was constantly after Rachel, raising a sharp storm about her ears. Father said the witch at once assumed the voice and tone of his stepmother, and got after Rachel. 'Tut, tut, Rachel, what makes you do so,' imitating grandmother exactly."

*Did your father ever speak of meeting the witch doctors and conjurers at Bell's?*

"Oh yes, ever so many came, and father used to tell many ridiculous and laughable incidents regarding the experiments of witch killers. The Bells allowed everyone who came along to experiment to his full satisfaction, and the witch always got the best of them. I remember one incident that amused him very much. This fellow put some silver, twelve dollars, in a bowl of water, performed his incantations, and set the bowl away, that the silver might remain in the water all night to work the enchantment when the witch came. Betsy Bell had to drink the enchanted water. Next morning the money was gone, which caused a mighty stir. A Negro was charged with stealing the money, and Mr. Bell was threatening the servant with a whipping. This was one of the times that Kate came to the Negro's rescue. 'Hold on, old Jack,' spoke Kate, 'that Negro is innocent; I can tell you who got that money,' and did tell. Mr. Bell dropped the matter and said no more about it. Several evenings later father went over to entertain the witch while the family and visitors slept. After all had retired and everything was quiet, father said he sat leaning his chair against the wall, waiting for Kate. Presently he felt something touch him on the shoulder, and he was directly accosted by the voice of the witch. 'Say Jack, did you hear about that money scrape they had here the other evening?' 'Yes,' replied father, 'I heard something about it.' 'Well, it was funny; I saved that nigger from a good whipping by telling old Jack who got the money,' and then went on to state that the person who got the money went to Spring field yesterday and bought lots of nice things with it. 'Ha, ha, ha, I guess they will quit fooling with these witch doctors now.' Father had occasion to go to Springfield a day or two later, and inquired about the transactions of this per son as told by Kate, and found that the witch had reported correctly."

*Did you, Mrs. Ayers, ever hear Bennett Porter say anything about the witch?*

"No; Bennett Porter moved away while I was quite a child. I have, however, heard various persons say that Bennett Porter shot at the witch, and it made much ado about it, threatening something serious to him or his children. I have also heard it repeated by many that the witch was seen by Betsy swinging on the limb of a tree and looking like a little girl dressed in green."

*Did you ever hear Williams or Joel Bell express any opinion in regard to the witch?*

"Nothing particular. They discussed it in a general way when asked questions regarding the demonstrations, but never seemed disposed to talk much about it. I suppose they had heard enough of it. However, Joel told me that the witch gave him the severest whipping he ever felt, and one that he would never forget as long as he lived."

*Mrs. Ayers, did you ever hear anything detrimental in any way to the character of John Bell or his family?*

"Not a breath in the world. No man or family stood higher in the estimation of the people than John Bell. I have heard him spoken of as one of the leading men of the country, and father said the citizens had the utmost confidence in his integrity. More than that, he raised his children to be honorable men and women, and the family influence is felt in Robertson county to this day; even the grandchildren are men of the same substantial character."

*Do you remember anything about Rev. Thomas and Rev. James Gunn?*

"Yes, certainly; they were the founders of Methodism in this section, and Rev. Sugg Fort was the leading Baptist. Their lives were full of good works and honors. I have heard it said many times that they visited Mr. Bell often and sympathized with him in his distress."

# Chapter 14

## Testimonials: The Bell Family, the Gunns, Forts, Johnsons, Porters, Frank Miles and Other Citizens Whose Statements Authenticate the History of the Bell Witch

Rev. Joshua W. Featherston, of Cedar Hill, Tenn., who after a long and useful career retired from the ministry and now lives happily, himself and wife, at his cottage, honored by all people, writes as follows:

CEDAR HILL, TENN, Dec. 23, 1891

In answer to the request to contribute what I know in regard to the characters or standing of Rev. Thomas Gunn, Rev. James Gunn, Rev. Sugg Fort, John and Calvin Johnson, W. B. Porter, Frank R. Miles, and the Bell family, I will state that they were among the early settlers of Robertson county, Tenn. I was intimately acquainted with each and every one of them except old Mr. John Bell, who died just before I settled in the neighborhood, and it is with pleasure that I can testify to their, high characters as men of worth and standing in the community. They were men of undoubted honor, possessing strong minds, and were not easily imposed upon.

As to the subject in hand, the Bell Witch, the history of which is made up from the detailed statements of these men, in connection with others, I can say that I have had many conversations with the parties in regard to the matter, and they all testified to very nearly the same facts and details, and I believe every word they told me respecting the demonstrations. As regards Rev. James and Rev. Thomas Gunn, they did more towards the establishment of the Methodist church in this country than any other men. In fact they were the founders of Methodism in this and surrounding counties, and their influence is felt to this day. They married at least two-thirds of the couples, and preached nearly all the funerals, in this and surrounding country during many years, and finally went down to their graves in peace, ripe with age and full of honors.

—J. V. FEATHERSTON

The writer had an interesting interview with Rev. J. W. Featherston at his pleasant home, since the above letter was written. He repeats many thrilling incidents told him by the men above mentioned, all of which is found in other testimony. Mr. Featherston says he had more talk with Frank Miles in regard to the actions of the witch than any one else, and had implicit confidence in Miles as a man who would not exaggerate or misstate the truth. Miles weighed about two hundred and fifty pounds, was in the prime of life, vigorous and very stout. He was at John Bell's a great deal, going as other friends to relieve and comfort the family in their distress, just as he would have attended a sick neighbor. Mr. Miles had a lively experience with the witch, which required more courage than force to meet. He undertook to resist the playful frolics of the intruder, which rather excited the animus of the monster with resentment and pique for Miles, and it manifested special delight in snatching the cover from his bed and striking him heavy blows. Mr. Miles said he exercised all the strength in his arms in trying to retain the bed covering when the witch was pulling at it, but in vain; it was like tearing the whole fabric into shreds. Mr. Featherston further states that the witch sensation was the exciting theme of the whole community when he moved in, and continued so for years. It was the subject of discussion in every household, and is often talked of now, having a bearing upon other things.

One of the most remarkable features in the development of the witch character was its preeminent knowledge of men, an innate, tangible comprehension of every man's attributes of mind and nature. Every citizen or stranger that came in contact with the mystery found disparagement in trying to cope with it on any subject, and suffered, an exposure of the inmost purposes and secrets of the heart. Take for an example of its exposition of this supernatural gift, the Johnson brothers. There was no difference in their standing as men of high honor and integrity of char acter. John was perhaps considered the most intellectual and forcible man of the two, while Calvin was noted for his frankness, devotion to principle, and absolute freedom from all deceit and guile. These elements the witch observed, and while it manifested the highest pleasure in vociferating and palavering with John, it trusted Calvin implicitly, and assigned its reason for this distinction. Calvin, it said, was a pure, truthful, scrupulous, Christian man, and therefore it gave him its hand, which it refused John and everyone else, trusting no man as it did Calvin Johnson. On the other hand it characterized John as a sharp, unscrupulous, tricky man, "whose inmost purpose was to catch it," and this, so far as the witch was concerned, John admitted to be true, and that he had pursued unawares every scheme, plan, stratagem, artifice or illusion he was capable of inventing in his efforts to detect the author of these most miraculous demonstrations, and at last gave it up in despair, as a matter beyond human power, knowledge or comprehension. This one instance of distinguishing the difference in the characters of the Johnson brothers would not be sufficient basis for a settled conclusion that the so-called witch was an agency above human genius or power, but the same wonderful intuition, instinct and archness [sic] was developed in hundreds of instances, and was a leading characteristic in all of its operations, and for this reason Mr. Featherston says he cannot believe that the demonstrations were the result of any human agency.

## Dr. J. T. Mathews Testifies

Dr. J. T. Mathews, who has been a well established practicing physician of Cedar Hill for many years, writes as follows:

CEDAR HILL, TENN., Dec. 23, 1891
In answer to questions concerning the character of certain gentlemen among the older settlers, it gives me pleasure to testify to the high standing and stability of character concerning Frank R. Miles and W. B. Porter, whom I was personally acquainted with, but too young to remember the others. They were regarded as honorable gentle men, whose statements concerning any matter were to be relied upon implicitly without the least hesitation. They lived on Sturgeon Creek, were of the best families in their day and time, were known far and near, and no one who knew them would think of calling their veracity in question.
Respectfully,
J. T. MATHEWS

## E. Newton Knew the Men

Mr. E. Newton, an old and respected citizen of Cedar Hill, writes under date of Dec. 23, 1891:

I was personally acquainted with Rev. Thomas Gunn, Rev. James Gunn, William Porter, John Johnson, Calvin Johnson, Alexander Gunn, and the Bell family. They were of the best families that ever lived in this country, men of the highest integrity and were honored by all people. They were among the pioneers of civilization: and Christianity, and were the leaders in the development of the county. They molded the character of the best element now in this section, and their influence will live to affect generations to come. No men contributed more to the advancement of Christianity than the two Gunns.

—E. NEWTON

## A Host of Good Citizens Testify

To Whom It May Concern:

We, the undersigned, affix our names to this, understanding its full purport and intent, which is to certify that the following named men, to wit: Rev. James Gunn, Rev. Thomas Gunn, Alexander Gunn, Rev. Sugg Fort, John Johnson, Calvin Johnson, Frank R. Miles, Wm. B. Porter and John Bell, Sr., were among the first settlers of the western part of Robertson county, Tenn. They were all men of prominence and great influence, and their memories are respected and revered to this day by the descendants of all who knew them. Many of their descendents are now among us, honored and respected citizens. The men above named all lived to a ripe old age, and left behind them honored names, and we consider anything emanating from any of them as entirely trustworthy. The post office address of the signers to this is Cedar Hill, Tenn.

This Dec. 23, 1891.

*J. E. Ruffin*
*R. H. Bartlett*
*H. B. Spain*
*A. L. Bartlett*
*L. Batts*
*J. W. M. Gooch*
*Matt. Gooch*
*Mrs. T. J. Ayers*
*W. R. Featherston*
*William Wvnn*
*E. S. Hawkins, M. D.*
*B. H. Sory, Sheriff*
*R. S. Draughon*
*B. S. Byrns*
*W. J. Barnes*
*J. H. Long, Jr.*

G. W. Sherod
Levi Dunn
W. H. Menees
H. W. Williams
A. L. Batts.
A. J. Newton
William Soloman
R. B. Long
R. B. Morris
E. W. Gunn
J. T. Bartlett
Mary A. Bartlett
Nannie M. Morriss
W. L. Melon
J. R. Rufffin
G. M. Darden
D. P. Ayres
Mrs. M. L. Ayers
J. H. Long, Sr.
W. J. Darden
J. C. Davis
M. J. Batts
T. B. Polk
J. H. Wynn
T. D. Morris
G. B. Fyke
C. B. Darden

## Major Garaldus Pickering, the Man
## Who Kicked the Witch out of Bed

Mr. R, H. Pickering, an honored citizen of Clarksville, Tenn., who has been connected with the business interest of the city for forty years, also served as County Trustee, and is a prominent official in the Methodist Church, known throughout the Tennessee Conference, contributes the statement of his father, Major Garaldus Pickering, who was a distinguished citizen of his day, and visited the Bell family during the witch excitement. No testimony could be more reliable, Mr. Henry Pickering states:

> I have heard my father, Garaldus Pickering, tell many wonderful things about the Bell Witch. He taught a large school in the Bell vicinity for a number of years, and edu-

cated two or three of the Bell boys. He visited the family and had some experience with the witch, as it was called, though he did not believe in witchcraft, and said he was never afraid of it. He had no idea as to what it was, but certainly it was an insoluble mystery, which has never been accounted for. A great many people went to hear it talk and witness its tricks; strangers came from North Carolina, Virginia and other States, and it was nothing uncommon to find the stables and lots full of horses, and a horse tied in every corner of the lane fence.

Father told me some remarkable experiences that Frank Miles had with the witch, but I will only repeat one or two things in his own personal experience and contact. He said: The family and company had all retired for the night in the usual way. Presently he felt the cover slipping off toward the foot of the bed, and he drew it up, holding it tightly. The next minute he felt something like a hand or fingers tickling him under the toes. He drew his feet up and kicked with all the power in him. He felt something weighty as his feet struck it, and heard it strike against the wall and fall to the floor, making a noise more like the falling of a side of heavy sole leather, than anything he could describe.

Another instance; while the family and guests were at supper, the subject of a wedding that was to take place at that hour came up. Father stated the names of the contracting parties, which I have forgotten, but remember the circumstance very distinctly, as it impressed me at the time. However, someone remarked that the hour for the marriage had about passed, and the parties were no doubt then man and wife. Another remarked that Rev. Gunn performed the ceremony. The witch then spoke, exclaiming, "No, he did not marry them."

"Yes, but you are mistaken this time," replied one. "Brother Gunn was engaged to tie the knot, and he never fails."

"He failed this time," returned the witch. "Brother Gunn was taken very sick and could not go, and the wedding was about to be a failure, but they sent off for Squire Byrns and he married them." No one present believed it possible for the witch to know the facts so soon, but this was ascertained on the following day to be the truth of the case in every particular. Regarding the authorship of these very singular exhibitions, father thought it absurd to charge it to any of the Bell family. They were the sufferers, and suffered greatly; moreover, they were everyone afraid of it; that was clear to any observer. He was there one night when several strangers rode up and hallooed ever so long, and not one of the family could be induced to go out, because they were afraid, and he got out of bed, dressed, and went out himself.

## John A. Gunn's Statement

CLARKSVILLE, TENN., May 16, 1893
To the Author —
Dear Sir:

In reply to your questions I will state that I am familiar with the Bell Witch story as written by Richard Williams Bell, and that I have heard the same things that are detailed by him, and many other incidents not recorded, repeated over and again by the old citizens who lived in the vicinity at that time. I have heard my father, Alexander Gunn, John Johnson and Frank Miles all repeat the circumstance of finding the vial of poison in the cupboard at the time of John Bell's death, the experiment in giving it to a cat, etc., just as told by the writer, all three being present and witnessed Mr. Bell's death and the circum. stances. I have heard Calvin Johnson tell the circumstance of his shaking hands with the witch, and many other very strange things. I have heard my grandfathers, Rev. James Gunn and Rev. Thomas Gunn, repeat many of the demonstrations which came under their observation; also James Johnson related the same things; the story of the witch bringing Mrs. Lucy Bell grapes and hazelnuts. Mrs. Martha Bell, wife of Jesse Bell, who lived to be ninety-six years of age; told me the story regarding the stockings as written by Williams Bell. Also I have heard William Porter repeat the same circumstance of the witch's visit to his house and getting in bed with him. I have heard Alex Gooch and wife, who was Theny Thorn, Jeff. and James Gooch, Jerry Batts, Major Robert Bartlett, Prof. John D. Tyler, of Montgomery County, and many others who witnessed the demonstrations, relate the same events and discuss many other things observed. I have also talked with Mrs. Betsy Powell regarding her troubles with the mysterious visitation. All of these people lived to a good old age, James Johnson passed his ninety-ninth year, John Johnson passed eighty, Grandfather Thomas Gunn ninety-six, and Rev. James Gunn seventy years. They were all honored citizens, whose statements were trustworthy in regard to any matter, and no one who ever knew them doubted the truth of the circumstances regarding the witch demonstrations at John Bell's and other places in the neighborhood. Moreover, these citizens followed every clue, exercised all of their wits, applied all manner of tests, placed unsuspected detectives in and around the house, acted upon all suggestions regarding the suspicion that had been lodged against certain members of the family, and with all, their investigations ended in confusion, leaving the affair shrouded in still deeper mystery, which no one to this day has ever been able to account for or explain in any intelligent or satisfactory way. Besides the names I have mentioned among the most prominent citizens of the community, hundreds of men from other communities and sections visited the place, remaining days and nights, for the same purpose, and all failed in the object of detecting the cause of the demonstrations.

John Johnson, perhaps, took more interest in the investigations than any other man; in fact, from all I could gather, he was the leader and inventor of most all the schemes resorted to. He was a man of splendid endowments, keen observation, quick perception, and close comprehension; self-willed, and self-possessed, sustaining an unsullied and intrepid character. Moreover, he was less given than most of men to the superstitious ideas that characterized the people in that age, and as he told me, he entered into the investigation believing that some human agency was at the bottom of the strange manifestations, and he was determined to find it out if possible.

Knowing Mr. Johnson and others who lived long years ago, as I did, together with the statements of my father and grandfather, I cannot at all question the appearance and existence of the unsolved mystery of the Bell Witch, nor do I doubt the actual occurrence of the incidents recorded by Richard Williams Bell, whom I knew to be one of the purest and best of men that ever lived in Robertson County.

Respectfully,
JOHN A. GUNN

## David Thompson Porter's Testimony

Esquire Zopher Smith, a prominent Magistrate of Clarksville, Tenn., was raised in Keysburg, Ky., and gratefully remembers David Thompson Porter as the friend of his youth. Mr. Porter was a merchant of Keysburg, and was honored for his worth as a citizen of the highest integrity and force of character, enjoying at that day a reputation Similar to that sustained by his distinguished son, Dr. D. T. Porter, of Memphis, Tenn. Squire Smith was a young clerk in the store, and he says he has heard Mr. Porter state repeatedly that he spent many nights at John Bell's, acting in concert with other citizens in trying to detect the agency of those most mysterious and wonderful demonstrations, following up every clue, and exhausting all resources and stratagems to no purpose. Squire Smith recounts many incidents stated by Mr. Porter, which impressed him at the time, especially the story of the witch carrying hazelnuts and grapes to Mrs. Bell, which Mr. Porter said was a positive fact. He described the knocking at the door like someone seeking admittance, and instantly the door would open of its own accord, and then the witch would begin talking. He also described the pulling of the cover off of the beds, and nearly all of the characteristic incidents recorded by Williams Bell, which need not be repeated. Such statements as this are of course hearsay, or second-handed testimony, but nevertheless reliable. The writer has several times observed Squire Smith as a witness in s higher court, testifying to the preliminary statements of certain witnesses in his court, which was accepted as valid testimony, and this is just the same kind of evidence. The men and Women of mature years who witnessed the demonstrations have all passed away, but we have the incidents recorded by Williams Bell, and approved by other members of the family, who were living witness to all of it, and these hearsay statements are simply repetitions of the same facts by other parties who never saw Williams Bell's manuscript, or knew that such a record was in existence, and the chain of evidence is as complete and strong as it is possible to make any kind of testimony. Squire Smith says Mr. Porter affirmed his statements with the same emphasis as if he had been qualified in a court of justice, and he could not disbelieve a word he said.

## Dr. William Fort's Investigation

The writer is authorized by a highly reputable lady of the Fort connection to state that Dr. William Fort came all the way from his home, then in Missouri, to investigate the phenomena. Parties who had failed in all of their efforts to explain the mystery, gave publicity to the suspicion that the demonstrations had their origin in the practices of ventriloquism by certain members of the family (something that would have been impossible without the knowledge of the old people and intimate neighbors, and without easy detection).

Dr. Fort determined to make a thorough test of this version, and had the accused members to sit by him, holding his hands over their mouths while the witch continued to talk uninterrupted and without change or modulation in the tone of voice.

## Private Conversation Exposed

The same lady relates this incident: Jesse Herring and wife were two estimable old people who lived in the vicinity. They were extremely cautious and guarded in their conversation about other people, and never discussed the witch or spent any opinion about it away from their own fireside. One night with closed doors, and not a soul in the house except themselves, they discussed the mystery very freely, and not a word was spoken by either of them to any one in regard to this conversation, or the witch. On the following night the witch reported to be whole conversation to the company assembled at John Bell's.

## Emptied the Milk Vessels

Mrs. Betsy Sugg called one morning to pay Mrs. Lucy Bell a visit. The subject of milk and butter came up, and Mrs. Bell spoke of her new dairy house and invited Mrs. Sugg out to show her how nicely it was arranged. She had just finished straining and setting the milk for cream, locked the door and put the key in her pocket. The milk was set in pewter basins, vessels then in common use for milk, with wooden covers. Mrs. Bell took the key from her pocket, unlocked and opened the door, and to her surprise and chagrin there was not a drop of milk there, and the basins were turned bottom up and the covers placed over them. "Some of Kate's mischief," exclaimed Mrs. Bell. "The witch is always playing some such prank as this."

## Uncle to the Devil

The witch it is said always treated the preachers, the Gunns and Rev. Sugg Fort, with more respectful consideration than other people. It was inclined to be on intimate or jocular terms with Rev. Fort, calling him Uncle Suggie, always welcoming him at the door with a happy salutation, "Good morning," or "Good evening Uncle Suggie. How do you like to be called uncle to the devil ?"

## Frightened Jerry Stark's Horse

Mr. James Chapman, a good citizen of Keysburg, Ky., spent the prime of his life in Robertson County, and repeats many of the incidents herein noted, as he heard them stated by older citizens. He heard more from Jerry Stark than any other person, and says, knowing the upright character of the man, he could not question Mr. Stark's statements. Mr. Stark visited the Bell place frequently during the witch excitement, and the progress of the investigations, and generally stayed all night.

Mr. Stark, says Chapman, described a large tree that stood in the Bell lane, under which he had to pass, when leaving the Place the following morning, after staying over night, and invariably, as he approached near, a rustling sound was heard among the leaves of the tree, and immediately as he passed under the tree, something apparently the size of a rabbit would jump out of the tree behind him, and that instant his horse would dash off as fast as he could go, which Mr. Stark said he could not account for, and never saw anything more of the spectre after it jumped. Mr. Chapman further states that some time after the old Bell house had been torn away, he was there helping Williams Bell in the wheat harvest. The grain was very rank, and they had stopped under a pear tree to whet their scythes and rest, and while there he mentioned this circumstance as told him by Mr. Jerry Stark, and Williams Bell confirmed the statement, pointing to the tree which was still standing, remarking that Stark's horse always started in a run with him the moment he passed under that tree.


## Esquire James I. Holman Writes

SPRINGFIELD, TENN., Nov. 4, 1893
M. V. Ingram —
My Dear Sir:

I see in the Nashville Banner of November 3d, a statement to the effect that you are writing a history of the Bell Witch for publication, and I write you to say that I want a copy as soon as it is out. I am now fifty-one years of age, and have as keen a relish for reading the full details of the great mystery as I did when a boy, and heard my grandfather, Irvin Polk, tell so much of the many wonderful things he had witnessed, known as the witch demonstrations. He lived near the Bell place, and was there on many occasions and witnessed strange things that he could in no way account for, and which, as I. understand, has never been explained. I could not doubt the statements of grandfather, even had I never heard them confirmed by many others, and it certainly was a wonderfully mysterious thing. The old Bell house in which the witch performed, if you do not know the fact, was many years ago torn down and moved to the place on the bluff of Brown's ford, now occupied by Levi Smith and family. I learn from my father, Col. D. D. Holman, that Major Wash. Lowe, who you remember as a prominent lawyer of Springfield, undertook to write up the facts, but for some reason never finished, and turned his writing over to Allen Bell, which you may get and learn something from.

  Respectfully, your friend,
  JAMES I. HOLMAN

  The writer will state that he has all the notes written by Major Lowe, but it is so badly faded and colorless that very little of it is legible.

## William Wall's Experience With the Witch

Esquire J. E. Ransdell, of the Fourteenth District of Montgomery County, Tenn., relates the experience of Uncle Billy Wall with the witch, as he heard the old gentleman tell it to many persons. Mr. Wall lived at Fredonia, in Montgomery County. He has been dead some ten years, but his story impressed Squire Ransdell in such a way that he has never forgotten it. Uncle Billy said he concluded to go over to Bell's and hear the mysterious talking that was exciting the country. He started late, on a good fat horse, that was remarkable for its good saddle qualities and gentleness. Nearing the place he was hailed by a voice, in the bushes calling him familiarly, "Hello, Billy Wall, you are going to see the witch?"

  "Yes", replied Uncle. Billy, "that is where I am going." The voice replied, "I am going there too, and believe I will ride behind you on that fat horse."

  "All right," returned Mr. Wall, "hop up." That moment he felt his horse squat, as if some heavy weight had fallen upon him, and then commenced wriggling, prancing and kicking up. He threw one hand behind to feel what it was, and then the other hand, but found nothing, and yet, he said, "the damn thing kept up a continual palavering at my back, asking me all sorts of hell-fired questions, while my horse continued in a canter, squealing and kicking up, and every damn hair on my head stood straight up, reaching for the treetops. It wasn't any fun for me, but the damn thing kept on laughing and talking about my fine race horse, and how pleasant it was to ride behind on his broad fat back, telling me what a fine suit of hair I had, and how beautifully it stood up, making me look like a statesman. I let my horse out, and wasn't long in getting there. As soon as I halted in front of the house, the damn thing politely invited me to 'light Mr. Wall, hitch your horse to the rack and go in; I will be in pretty soon and entertain you.' Just about an hour later the racket commenced, and it looked like hell was to pay. It came rattling like dried hazelnuts pouring down by showers on the floor; and all sorts of talking going on. That trip satisfied me; I got enough of the witch in one night and never went back."

Squire Ransdell says the way in which Mr. Wall told this story, giving emphasis to nearly every word, portraying in expression his own feelings at the time, was the most laughable thing he ever heard.

## Joshua Gardner Testified to the Wonderful Phenomena

Among the many letters in answer to the advertisement for the Bell Witch, after it went into the hands of the publisher, the following from W. H. Gardner, a prominent business man of Union City, Tenn., and A. E. Gardner, of Dresden. Tenn., a gentleman favorably known throughout the State for his high integrity, presents evidence regarding Joshua Gardner's experience with the witch demonstrations:

UNION CITY, TENN., April 20, 1894
M. V. Ingram —
Dear Sir:
    When will your book, "History of the Bell Witch," be out? My uncle, Joshua Gardner, was a conspicuous figure in the remarkable affair, as Betsy Bell's lover, and of course I want to read your history. Truly, as you say, it is the most wonderful phenomenon that ever occurred in this or any other country, and which will no doubt ever remain a mystery. I can recall, perhaps, an hundred occasions since I was a boy that I heard Uncle Joshua relating the remarkable story, and strange: to say, in the latter years of his life, he was loath to speak of it, even when urged to recount the queer

doings and sayings of the witch, and then, if one of his hearers manifested the least inclination to disbelieve, he would desist. He believed in it as strong as he held to his religion, and a more devoted, conscientious Christian man never lived than Joshua Gardner. He died a few years since at the age of eighty-four years. I remember that Uncle Joshua received a copy of the Philadelphia Saturday Evening Post of 1849, containing a long and interesting account of the witch, written by a reporter. We kept the paper until a few years since, but it has in some way been lost and cannot now be found. I understand that Mrs. Wade, living near here, who is now ninety years of age, was a witness to the stirring and exciting incidents. There are several persons in this vicinity who are familiar with the history of the witch, and agree perfectly as to the facts of the remarkable phenomenon.

Respectfully,
W. H. GARDNER

DRESDEN TENN., April 25, 1894

M. V. Ingram —

Dear Sir:

I see notice of your intention to publish a history of the "Bell Witch." My uncle, Joshua Gardner, figured considerably in the life of the witch, and of course I have heard a great deal about it and feel anxious to see the history, and will ask you to put me down as one of your first subscribers.

Respectfully,
A. E. GARDNER

# Chapter 15

## *Latest Demonstrations:*
## *The Witch's Return After Seven Years*

Williams Bell says when the witch took its departure in 1821, bidding adieu to the family, it promised to return in seven years. He also records the fact that it did return according to promise, remaining some two weeks, making the same demonstrations that characterized the first appearing, and that himself, Joel Bell and their mother, Mrs. Lucy Bell, were the only members of the family then remaining at the old homestead — John, Drew and Betsy, those accused of producing the demonstrations, having all gone away to themselves, and were not apprised of the reappearance, the three having agreed to keep the matter a profound secret, lest the old troubles should be renewed. This statement is substantiated by Joel, who in later years never hesitated to talk about the family troubles, detailing the circumstances to interested friends inquiring into the mystery. He consulted with his brother in regard to the publication, read his manuscript, and knew everything that was in it. Williams Bell, however, does not vouch for the many reports of strange noises and varied sounds, and mysterious appearances, seen and heard about the place and at several other places in that end of the county, to which others testify; much of the testimony to these apparitions has been omitted. He heard no more of it up to the date of his writing, 1846. Later than this, however, there is some well substantiated evidence to demonstrations similar to the early manifestations.

After the death of Mrs. Lucy Bell, the land was divided, and Joel received the river plot, adjoining Williams on the north, on which he settled after his marriage.

## *Dr. Henry H. Sugg's Statement*

Dr. Henry H. Sugg's statement is first of importance, which the writer is authorized to repeat by three highly creditable persons, one a lady, and the others, Col. Thomas Trigg, of Montgomery County, Tenn., and Mr. John A. Gunn, to whom he made the statement at different times, and all repeat it precisely alike; also Col. Yancey narrates the same story. Dr. Sugg said he was called to Joel

Bell's to see a sick child. This was about 1852. It was a cold day, and entering the house as usual he found a comfortable fire burning, and placing his medical pocket on the floor by the door as he entered, he seated himself by the fire to warm. Immediately he heard a rapping or rattling of glass in the valise, and instantly following this was an explosive sound like the popping of corks, and a crash of the vials. He was sure that every bottle in the valise had been smashed, and he jumped up excitedly to ascertain the cause, but on opening the valise, found nothing out of place and no harm done. Mr. Bell also observed the same thing, and remarked that such things were common, that he never paid any attention to them. This statement is further supported and given additional significance by:

## Reynolds Powell's Story

Reynolds Powell tells the story of a circumstance that occurred at the same place in 1861. Joel Bell sold this farm to his brother Williams, and after the death of Williams Bell, the place was allotted to his son, Allen Bell, who cultivated it several years before he was married.

The writer visited Mrs. Annie Powell, a daughter of the late Dr. Scott, of Barren Plains, Robertson County, and widow of DeWitt Powell, who now resides near Barren Plains, for the purpose of interviewing her on the subject in hand. We found her quite an interesting lady, familiar with the entire history of the Bell Witch, as she had heard it repeated by her father and mother, and mother-in-law, the Gunn family, and many others, rehearsing, as she did, many of the circumstances already recorded, remarking in the conversation, "Allen Bell could, tell you a very interesting circumstance if he would, but I have no idea that he will, as he has never spoken of it to any of us. Reynolds Powell, however, told all about the affair the next day after it happened. Allen Bell had about recovered from a hard spell of sickness. In fact he was discharged from the army soon after he joined on account of bad health, from which he was not expected to recover. Reynolds Powell went down to spend a night with him during his convalescence, and on his return home next morning he told how bad he and Allen were scared. Allen had been staying with his stepmother, but other company came in, and they went over to Allen's place to sleep, in order to make room. They retired, leaving the doors open for fresh air, and very soon, he said, the dog commenced barking furiously, and ran into the house greatly frightened, while a strange noise was heard without. The dog continued snarling, snapping and barking in a frightened way that indicated a close contest with something. They got up to see what was the matter, but could not discover anything unusual and put the dog out, closing the doors. The dog took to his feet and left the place, and all was quiet for the next hour, when they were awakened by the removal of the bolster from under their heads, and then followed the sheets, being jerked from under them. They arose to investigate the cause, but could find nothing out of the regular order of things. They replaced the sheet and bolster, securely bolted the doors, and retired again, placing a light cover over them. After some while the same trick was repeated, the cover bolster and sheet all being snatched from the bed. They replaced the things, which were removed the third time. They then placed the bolster on the bed, and laid with their breasts across it, holding with their hands, determined to retain it, but it was immediately snatched away with great force., and the bolster was thrown on top of their heads, and this ended the contest. He said they didn't sleep much, and I suppose that was true. You ask Allen about it."

Reynolds Powell was killed in the Confederate army after this. The Writer interviewed Allen Bell in regard to the circumstance, and he admitted that it was substantially true, but he was surprised to learn that Reynolds Powell had ever told it to any one. He said, however, that the demonstrations were never repeated while he remained on the place. This demonstration was characteristic of the performances at John Bell's, and was evidently the acts of the same agency.

Another characteristic incident in the same vicinity, or on the Bell place, several years later, to which reputable gentlemen testify, is here presented.

## Music of the Enchanted Spring

John A. Gunn and A. L. Bartlett testify that during the year 1866 they had occasion to cross Red River, and the stream having swollen too full for fording; they left their horses on the south, or Bell side of the river, and crossed over in a canoe. Returning late in the afternoon, they landed near the famous enchanted spring, designated by the spirit as the hiding place of the treasure trove. They did not land there, however, with any expectation of finding the treasure — oh no. They sought a cooling draught of limpid water to quench their burning thirst, so they say, which is evidently true. However, after refreshing themselves, they started up the hill, when a sweet strain of music pierced their ears like a volume of symphony vibrating the air. They both in voluntarily stopped, and seated themselves on a moss covered stone, listening to the ravishing melody which continued some thirty minutes. It was unlike any music they had ever heard. The modulating sound was indescribable, and unsurpassingly sweet. It was utterly impossible to discover from whence it came, the whole atmosphere seemed thrilled with vibrating euphony, and the gentlemen were caught up, as it were, on wings of ecstasy.

Heartless people who have no conception of the mysterious, no ear for music, no eye for the beautiful and no taste for the sweets of this life, ascribe such manifestations as this to the imagination under a peculiar state of mind, and bewildering circumstances. But not so in this case. These gentlemen were then in the vigor of young manhood, and had crossed the river that day in defiance of wind and wave to spend a joyous Sabbath with their best girls. Evidently they did not return with their hearts attuned to a heavenly sonnet, for neither of them married on the north side of the river, nor did they ever cross again on the same mission, and therefore could not have experienced the passionate throbbings that calls forth such an euphonious dulcet.

The writer can bear testimony to some remarkable experiences in crossing the same stream near the charmed spring, and it is under altogether different circumstances and state of mind that ones imaginations take flight, catching sweet intonations from the rippling waves, and chasing billows, bringing the cadence into diapason with the melody of the birds, and the chant of the sylph, forming a transporting consonance that carries the soul beyond that blessed abode where the ordinary mortal is willing to stop. These gentlemen had no such experience; in truth they sought a draught of lethe in all possible haste — a spring known to all lovers of that section as the gushing stream of oblivion, and he who drinks may depart in forgetfulness. Kate the spirit, is ever present to administer to the comfort of' a despairing swain. There was no circumstance attending this incident that could have possibly exercised the imagination. The gentlemen were tired and had no imagination, and there could not have been any illusion or delusion, in the melodious sound that pierced their ears. It was no other than Kate, the witch, who always put in just at the right time and place unexpectedly and most mysteriously, and no doubt that the sweet strains of music was very helpful to their fatigued feelings.

Be this as it may, they are men of veracity and testify to the truth of this incident. They were then fresh from the field of battle, familiar with the sound of rattling musketry and roaring cannon, and were not easily frightened or deceived. Kate was a musical witch, and the circumstance is characteristic of the acts performed years before.

The writer has information of two incidents which occurred in 1872, a few miles from the Bell place, that were of the same nature and character of the disturbances that annoyed the Bell family so much, and unmistakably emanated from the same source or agency. These demonstrations were witnessed by two young ladies who could not have been mistaken. But, for proper and prudent reasons, they request that the circumstances and details be omitted in this publication, and in deference to their wishes they are not recorded. However, these incidents are sufficient to enable the author to trace the operations, of the agency known as the "Bell Witch" from 1817 to 1872, a period of fifty-five years, and he leaves readers to form their own conclusion as to the nature and authorship of the demonstrations. The testimony presented is given on the authority and statements of the very best people of the country, men and women who would not tend their names and influence for the purpose of making up a story of fiction, and altogether goes to establish, beyond question or doubt the existence for fifty-five years of the greatest mystery and wonder that the world has any account of.

The writer has only to say in conclusion, that if it was the work of human agency, the author was a shrewd devil, of great age and wonderful cunning, to have escaped detection during so long a reign terrorizing the fears of timid people, continuing still at large undiscovered and unknown, in a country of sharp detectives, set to catch evil doers of every description. Conceding that it is possible for a person or persons, through any kind of mechanism, skill or human genius, to inaugurate such a mystifying terror, continuing over a half century undiscovered, is to admit that the present century of Christian civilization has progressed far beyond any other age in developing deviltry in human nature.